For my parents,
Peter and Barbara

A NEW LABOUR NIGHTMARE

THE RETURN OF THE AWKWARD SQUAD

ANDREW MURRAY

V

VERSO

London • New York

First published by Verso 2003
© Andrew Murray 2003
All rights reserved

1 3 5 7 9 10 8 6 4 2

Verso
UK: 6 Meard Street, London W1F 0EG
USA: 180 Varick Street, New York, NY 10014-4606
www.versobooks.com

Verso is the imprint of New Left Books

ISBN 1-85984-552-5

British Library Cataloging in Publication Data
A catalogue record for this book is available from the British Library

Library of Congress Cataloging-in-Publishing Data
A catalog record for this book is available from the Library of Congress

Typeset in Garamond
Printed in the UK by the Cromwell Press

Contents

PART TWO: AWKWARD VOICES

Preface

The subject matter of this book is the future of trade unionism in Britain. Since the British trade union movement was for many years held to be the most powerful in the world, the story of its dramatic fall, and the present possibility of its rising again, also have an international significance.

The book is based largely on interviews with the new generation of union leaders whose recent rise to influence has suggested that we may be on the threshold of a fresh start in trade unionism and labour politics more generally. The new leaders – dubbed the 'awkward squad' by the media, although it is a term some of them dislike – set out their views on the most pressing questions and outline their vision of the future.

To provide essential perspective, the first part of the book endeavours to explain how the trade union movement got from where it was – an apparently unchallengeable power in Britain in the early 1970s – to where it is today and sets out the political and industrial challenges it faces in the near future. This section includes interviews with Jack Jones and Ken Gill, two of the most eminent (and thoughtful) of the labour movement's leaders from that earlier period.

The second part consists of interviews with some of the key union figures of today and tomorrow, in which they address the issues confronting this potential union resurgence. Some of those interviewed are less well known than others, and there are a number of important figures in the movement whose views are not directly represented. However, those featured do between them cover the range of opinion within the left, and highlight the main issues which need to be considered. By way of an illustration of the possibilities of union struggle, an account of the little-noticed 'Battle of Dolphin Square' is also included.

While there is no common 'party line', the thrust of the interviews is without doubt a repudiation of the main elements of the strategy which has informed the trade union movement since the end of the great miners' strike of 1984–85. The era of 'social partnership' and 'New Labour' is drawing to a close, albeit painfully and fitfully. This is entirely welcome to the author and, as can be seen, to those others who present their views in these pages.

Acknowledgements

I have been lucky enough to spend nearly all my working life within the labour movement, so thanks are due to the three organisations which have employed me for the great bulk of the last twenty-six years – the *Morning Star* newspaper, the Transport and General Workers Union and the train drivers' union, ASLEF. Without that experience, I could not have attempted this book. Particular thanks to ASLEF and its general secretary, Mick Rix, who have once again been most supportive throughout the writing of this book.

Thanks also to Tariq Ali, Gavin Everall, Jane Hindle, Tim Clark and their colleagues at Verso, and to Seumas Milne and Anna Kruthoffer for many useful comments on the manuscript. Any errors and all opinions not otherwise ascribed are the author's own.

I am especially grateful to my children, Jessica, Jack and Laura, and my wife, Anna, for their support and encouragement. Finally, thanks to my parents, Peter and Barbara, to whom this book is dedicated.

PART ONE

Resuming the Forward March?

There are now two crucial questions facing this country: First, 12 years after Margaret Thatcher left the stage, how strong is the once-mighty trades union movement? Secondly... how great is Mr Blair's resolve?

Daily Mail, 27 November 2002

1

New Labour, Firefighters and War

It is summer 2003 and Britain is entering its seventh year of 'New Labour' government. The country is governed by a Home Secretary who regards 'liberal' and 'progressive' as terms of abuse; by a Chancellor bent on taking privatisation into areas the Conservatives never dreamed of, a man who prides himself on his parsimonious reputation, yet pledged to pay 'whatever it takes' to fund war; by a Health Secretary who declared that he saw no moral problem whatsoever in the Labour Party being funded by the proceeds of pornography in the form of donations from adult magazine proprietor Richard Desmond; and by a Deputy Prime Minister prepared to ban lawful industrial action by trade unionists in support of a pay claim.

And, finally, it is governed by Tony Blair, a man whose resolve on any matter touching on ruling-class interests is not really in any doubt, who is besotted by the rich, contemptuous of his own party, who continues to press forward a programme for a new 'moralising' British imperialism around the world, as second-in-command in an apparently endless series of US-led wars.

There have been worse governments in British history – Lord Liverpool's post-Napoleonic Wars administration, and Mrs Thatcher's more recent period in office are certainly contenders. But never has there been a more reactionary government rooted in and nourished by a labour movement – either in Britain itself or anywhere else in the developed industrial world.

The story of 'New Labour' is a unique passage in the political history of the worldwide working-class movement. It is the most explicit, indeed brazen, attempt to separate labour from its traditions of socialism, or even social justice, from any acknowledgement of a class divide in society, and in their place to embrace liberal economics, an authoritarian social policy and an imperialist world outlook.

Rooted in the experience of, and changes wrought by, Thatcherism in the 1980s, 'New Labour' is, however, now producing its own counter-reaction in turn. This is not being reflected in Ian Duncan-Smith's hapless Tories. No one should bet against an ultimate revival in the Conservative Party's fortunes, but on every issue exciting popular opposition to the Blair government, the Tories offer much the same policies without the premier's personal charm and presentational skills.

Never has parliamentary politics offered such a limited and sterile choice to the voters, who are showing their displeasure by abstaining from the electoral process in record numbers. Neither has such a large part of the population ever found itself holding views broadly to the left of a Labour government. Most people want the railways and other utilities to be brought back under public control; they want the gap between rich and poor narrowed, not widened; they oppose measures to privatise health and education; and they want a foreign policy based on peace and respect for international law, rather than subordination to the US far right.

The plain fact of British politics today is that if these views are to find a powerful voice, it must mainly be through the trade union movement, still the largest and deepest-rooted single social movement in the country. The trade unions have the greatest potential to be the real opposition to New Labour, at the heart of a broader alliance of all those discontented with the present government but aghast at the thought of any Tory return to office.

That is what politics needs. It is apparent that it is also what trade union members themselves want. The last two years have seen an almost unbroken run of victories in union elections for leaders who offer, to some degree or other, just that alternative. The carefully-cultivated 'moderation' of 1990s trade unionism is being rejected. Instead, overt opponents of Tony Blair and the whole thrust of his governing project are being elected. As one very senior union leader remarked a few months ago 'you can't be elected in a union as a Blair supporter today'.

The establishment, comfortable with a choice of 'New Labour' and old Tory at election time, is wise to the danger. Every newspaper has recently run photos and potted (often potty) biographies of the new union leaders – an 'awkward squad' of up-and-coming militancy, allegedly flexing their industrial muscles in the spirit of the 1970s.

Union power has become an issue once more. The bitter dispute between the Fire Brigades Union and the government over pay and cuts in the fire service in the winter of 2002–03 raised the controversy to a new pitch. Respectable opinion rallied to secure the ramparts of the Thatcher–New Labour political and economic system against the barbarians without.

However, there is still a sense that this may be an over-reaction. Is the revival in union power real? Is the political shift to the left in union elections matched by a resurgence in industrial influence? The facts, the first casualty of any tabloid press campaign, do not unambiguously bear this out; days lost to industrial action (although rising significantly) remain at low levels by the standards of pre-1990 decades and trade union membership is barely half what it was when Jim Callaghan lost his vote of confidence in the House of Commons in 1979 and as far as can be established, no retired generals are forming private armies in the countryside to maintain order and essential supplies in the event of a TUC-led coup – a staple of early-1970s upper-class agitation.

And yet, you don't have to wait until you are swept out to sea before you notice that the tide has turned. The sense that the 'forward march of labour', famously declared halted by the eminent historian Professor Eric Hobsbawm in 1978, might be on the point of resumption is not misplaced.

One week in July 2002 seemed to epitomise the new situation. In that week, a million local government workers took their first nationwide industrial action since 1979. A point of particular added significance was that this represented the largest single strike by women workers in British industrial history. That same week, amidst scenes of multiple-recount drama and 'will-he-won't-he-go' farce, worthy of a presidential election in Florida, Sir Ken Jackson lost his job at the head of amicus, Britain's biggest trade union in the private sector, to Derek Simpson, a relatively-unknown left-wing challenger. The particular significance of this was that the section of amicus voting in that election, the former Amalgamated Engineering and Electrical Union, has been *the* bastion of the right-wing in the trade union movement for generations.

After the defeat of Sir Ken, there could no longer be any doubt that there is a change in mood crossing all other barriers in the unions.

The election of Tony Woodley, a radical left-winger unafraid of industrial confrontation, to the leadership of the Transport and General Workers Union in June 2003 has confirmed the development.

It is not entirely one-way. Leading left-winger Mick Rix lost the leadership of ASLEF, to general surprise, in July 2003 – a defeat attributed to specific factors in the train drivers' union, energetically exploited by a well-organised and employer-supported right-wing. The lesson will not have been lost on others.

However, even these steps forward underline how much has changed since the 1970s. The local government strike, while strongly supported, did not have the effect on municipal services that it would have had thirty years earlier because so many of the functions of local government have been contracted-out to private companies, often employing casual staff. These are often beyond the reach of trade union organisation, in practice if not principle, and they were certainly legally-barred from supporting the strike action as a result of laws passed in the Thatcher–Tebbit years and carefully left in place since.

Nor could a change in leadership at the T&G or the AEEU have the immediate effect on industry that it would have had in the 1970s. So many of the industries and factories that defined the trade union movement and shaped its culture for so many years are no longer there.

If these changes and differences are to be addressed, the political and industrial struggles must be joined together within the trade union movement. Unlike any previous Labour government, Tony Blair's has widened inequality, allowed much of industry to go to the wall, and retained laws designed to weaken trade union organisation dramatically. It has also had as its cornerstone the reduction of trade union influence in the affairs of the Labour Party to a negligible level.

The clique of six or seven people, led by Tony Blair, who hijacked the Labour Party following John Smith's death in 1994 still dream of severing the historic connection between the unions and the party which they founded at the start of the twentieth century.

Events are making this a live issue once more – the unions are waking up politically. At Labour's 2002 conference, Blair was defeated for the first time on a matter of substance, when the major unions combined to demand a review of the policy of bringing profit-oriented finance into the running of major public services.

Still more strikingly, a number of trade unions, including Unison, the country's largest, joined the massive movement which grew up against Britain's support for George Bush's aggression against Iraq. On 15 February 2003, when two million people marched in London and Glasgow against the Prime Minister's neo-colonial war, the trade union leadership was in the forefront at the rallies (with the notable exception of the still-conservative TUC itself).

The anti-war movement extends far wider than the trade unions of course. But their strength as a force in society and their political role within the Labour Party added immense weight to the opposition to war – the more so, because unions have traditionally been slow to address sharp issues of foreign policy, as well as reluctant to challenge Labour politicians in this field.

And they went further. Shortly before the demonstration, the leaders of two important rail unions, Mick Rix and Bob Crow, said that it was time for Blair to resign as Prime Minister on the grounds that he has failed the country and split his party. That call has since been taken up by others.

The combination of the Iraq war and the firefighters' dispute has certainly undermined the Prime Minister's base of support within the labour movement. Many still shy away from logic and remain fearful of raising, or endorsing, the 'Blair must go' slogan. None, however, can provide any programme for changing government policy, and breaking 'New Labour's' death grip on the Party, that does not involve having the nerve to change the Prime Minister.

This is a new situation. Labour is being opposed from the left across the range of its policies, with most major trade unions and a host of smaller ones being at the very heart of that opposition. And Downing Street is fighting back, using all the well-practised techniques in its arsenal to discredit its critics: press attacks; intervention in union elections; attempts to divide the union leaderships are all being deployed. Of course, much of the establishment needs no prodding from Number Ten to go down the anti-left road. This has led to a rediscovery of some truths which previous generations of trade union activists would have held to be self-evident.

For example, if anyone had forgotten – or never known – just how much the British establishment hates and fears trade unionism, the firefighters' dispute of 2002–03 must have come as a shock. A visitor to a local fire station picket line was surprised when one of the fire-fighters expressed astonishment at the hostility shown to the union cause by the *Sun* newspaper. Surely everyone knew what attitude Rupert Murdoch's poisonous tabloid took towards strikes, the visitor thought.

In fact, if you came of age in the trade union movement after 1990 or thereabouts, there is no particular reason why you would. For more than ten years, assertive trade unionism was off the public radar. The war against organised labour, which dominated British politics for a generation, until around the late 1980s, appeared to be over, at least to the self-satisfied victors. The media and the Conservative Party regarded the unions as more-or-less finished business. With TUC-affiliated membership halved, socialism allegedly discredited (not least within the 'new' Labour Party) and the manager undisputed master in the workplace, it no doubt felt safe for the newspapers to declare victory and make their anti-union pundits with their venomous hostility stand down.

That started to change in 2002, with days lost to industrial action rising to a twelve-year high, including high-profile strikes in local government, on the railways and on London Underground – all of which attracted a very high degree of initial public support. But it was not until the firefighters' dispute began that the country could see just how much class hatred for trade unions still animates political and media circles. The *Sun* took the low road – personal abuse of Fire Brigades Union General Secretary Andy Gilchrist, harassment of his family and so on. The liberal wing of the establishment was little better. From his lofty perch at the *Guardian*, Hugo Young asserted that strong unions which pursue their own interests (what else might they do?) were nothing less than the enemies of political order. Martin Wolf in the *Financial Times* warned that if the firefighters achieved their pay demands, Britain would become ungovernable and would return to the 'anarchy' which he believes prevailed between 1969 and 1986.[1] Polly Toynbee expressed horror at the FBU's leadership and warned 'they will not win – not a chance'.[2] All of this was, of course, stoked by Downing Street's spin machine, which had earlier branded the union's leaders as 'Scargillites' who had to be 'crushed'.

By this time, the issue was whether the firefighters should be paid an extra 11 per cent or an extra 16 per cent in return for a variety of reforms, presented as 'modernisation' but in reality consisting of job cuts and longer hours. In June 2003 a settlement of the dispute was finally reached. Behind the straightforward industrial question at the core of the dispute, however, a larger issue clearly lurked. The 'union' of those who have prospered directly or indirectly from the diminution of the labour movement started to sense the possibility of the trammelling of the power they have enjoyed so munificently for the last fifteen years or so. When other union leaders expressed support for the FBU in the midst of the dispute, the *Sun* declared: 'It's A Class War.'[3]

'It certainly looks like one', I wrote in the *Guardian* at the time. '"Can't win, musn't win"' has been the refrain from the Cabinet to the Bank of England, from New Labour to old Tory, from Murdoch tabloids to *bien pensant* pundits. The FBU has been up against an axis of privilege, a common front of all those whom the perversities of the prevailing free market reward beyond reason, determined to defend themselves against those at the opposite end of the scale. Twenty-four years after the winter of discontent, seventeen years on from the miners' strike, the great and the good and the simply filthy rich still, more than anything else, fear the rise of the trade union movement from its slumbers. They are all Thatcherites now.'[4]

Presumably the dramatic reaction to the fire dispute was itself a product of shock at having to re-conquer an adversary which the rich and powerful thought was dead and buried. But if the 'class war' is back on again, who is going to win it? 'Back to the 1970s' may serve the tabloids as a shock headline, but it is not an attractive slogan for the labour movement. Nor is it a feasible one. The culture which nourished the long ascent of trade unionism has been decimated – industries have gone, the workforce has changed, the connection between work and community has often been uprooted – and that clock cannot be turned back. Many would not wish it to be – there is little reason for women workers or black Britons to look back on the

1960s and 1970s with nostalgia, and for the young, of course, it is the proverbial foreign country where things are done differently. Even if, on balance, life was more stable and secure, and increasing prosperity more assured for millions of people in those decades than it was before or has been since, those social gains can never now be restored on their former basis. There has been a vast global recomposition of capital in the last twenty years. The British working class, like its European counterparts, has changed as a consequence.

The challenge for the rising radicalism in the trade union movement today is whether it can help in the creation of a new culture of militancy and progress which, while drawing on the best traditions of working-class struggle, can also fit with the times. It is perhaps inevitable that the trade union movement will recover somewhat from its 1990s nadir, but nothing guarantees a definite return to its size and influence of earlier decades, let alone an even better future. The jury is out.

The crisis in trade unionism is an international phenomenon. While there are a host of organisational, political, cultural and even religious differences between the forms of trade unionism in developed capitalist countries, it is common to nearly all of them that their strength waxed for thirty years after the Second World War and has waned unevenly since. The common factors have been, broadly, the expansion and then contraction of mass-organised factory production as a share of the economic whole, and the expansion of the service sector and contracted-out and smaller-scale forms of labour organisation (if not of capital organisation, which is ever more centralised). The challenges which British labour faces in asserting security and dignity at work and attaining larger social objectives are common to the trade union movements of Europe, North America and elsewhere.

What the unions in Britain do now in the political field will also have worldwide resonance. New Labour has presented itself as the new template for the 'centre-left' and as a worldwide model for social democracy. Its defeat in the British labour movement would be a service to the international working-class movement, too, some would say to the world itself.

Tony Blair is above all a war premier; he has used British armed forces, usually outside international law and always for purposes of aggression, five times in his period of office. He has wrapped this up in a rhetoric which harks back to nineteenth-century colonialism. His attacks – real and painful – on social justice in Britain are as nothing compared to the dangers of his foreign policy. Both policies, foreign and domestic, essentially serve the same interests – that of the rich and powerful in Britain and around the world. Britain's labour movement could make no greater contribution to the common good than bringing the Blair era to a close.

2

The End of the Magnificent Journey

When Francis Williams published his quasi-official history of the British trade union movement in 1954, he entitled it *Magnificent Journey: The Rise of the Trade Unions*.

The title encapsulated not just the outlook that informed the book, but the outlook that animated the labour movement of the time. Williams' work is replete with references to the trade union 'success story', to the unions as a 'new estate of the realm' and even to the 'ascending spiral of history' upon which the trade unions were travelling ever further towards the imposition of 'a pattern of moral values on industrial civilisation'.[5]

Subsequent developments endorsed these high-flown claims. Twenty years later, *Top of the Pops* hummed to the chorus of the Strawbs hit 'you can't get me, I'm part of the union' and few doubted that it expressed one of the great prevailing truths of British society at the time. The then leader of the Transport and General Workers Union, Jack Jones, was repeatedly referred to as the most powerful man in the country – a statement that was not true, but was certainly not seen as absurd either.

To anyone less than forty years old, these are evocations of a different world. There have been many important changes over the past quarter century, but none have had such a profound effect on the lives of so many as the sustained and deliberate drive to weaken and, if possible, destroy the trade union movement as a power in British life.

Francis Williams caught the spirit of his times just about right. The growth of trade union power had seemed inexorable, irresistible and inevitable for some years before 1954, welcomed by the labour movement itself, of course, and even apparently accepted with weary resignation by the establishment – something to be accommodated, and certainly not confronted.

Even in the most difficult years of the 1930s, trade unionism had been suffused by a belief, expressed in different ways by left and right within the movement, that it was the force of the future. Industrial development and the extension of trade union organisation within it stretched ahead indefinitely. This ever-growing power would in the view of Williams and others piece by piece impose a new order on society or, according to the more modest ambitions of some of its leaders, at least smooth away the rough edges of the old order – impose ethics over economics. The Fabian 'inevitability of gradualism' was the prevailing doctrine of the day in 1954 and remained so for a further generation.

In the 1960s and 1970s, trade unionism in Britain reached its zenith. It extended to almost all sections of industry, deep into the public services and, for the first time, to considerable numbers of white-collar workers in the private sector. The organisations of the unions touched almost every part of British economic and social life. The unions did not, today's mythology notwithstanding, run the country – nor did they aspire to do so. But the country could not easily be run against them.

This period is now represented as being some kind of alien takeover of British life, as if trade unions were not democratic organisations of working-class men and women, profoundly rooted in the communities and collective experiences created by industrial capitalism. Their ascendancy to a position of relative strength in society was a product of 150 years of struggle and owed its success to those virtues of self-sacrifice and self-discipline which middle-class opinion finds so laudable in the individual (or in the military) and so threatening when expressed by a working-class movement.

The advance can be measured in figures. The membership of unions affiliated to the Trades Union Congress reached six and a half million in 1920 before falling back to half that number in 1934, in the depths of the Great Depression. From then on the gradient was unerringly upwards, with the few declines in membership recorded being tiny and temporary. Membership reached four million in 1937, five million in 1941, six million in 1943, seven million by 1947 and eight million in 1952, when Francis Williams was surveying the 'magnificent journey'.

Thereafter the rate of growth slowed somewhat – a total TUC-affiliated membership of more than nine million was not registered until 1970. Extraordinarily, the ten million mark was surpassed the very next year. By the end of the decade more than thirteen million employees were organised in trade unions, over half the national labour force.[6]

The early years of this advance were marked by great battles to organise factories and secure recognition of the union from employers. By the 1970s, however, members were pouring into trade unions without any great exertion on the part of the organisation. A generation of near full employment and the buoying up of working-class confidence engendered by this circumstance (unique in the history of British capitalism) provided a step change to the 'inevitability of gradualism', at least in the industrial sector.

The advance of labour could be recorded in other ways as well. King George V was alarmed when Ramsay MacDonald formed the first ministry led by the Labour Party in 1924. His apprehensions were, of course, unfounded. By the time MacDonald broke up the second Labour administration in 1931 to form the National (in effect Conservative) government, Labour's erstwhile hero was boasting that 'every Duchess in London will want to kiss me tonight'. But in 1940, Labour was restored to government under Churchill, with the founder and General Secretary of the T&G, Ernest Bevin, drafted in as Minister for Labour to supervise wartime mobilisation. Bevin had earlier reminded the world that the Labour Party had 'emerged from the bowels of the trade union movement'. It is because Bevin's inelegant formulation was essentially true that Hartley Shawcross's famous declaration – 'we are the masters at the moment, and not only at the moment, but for a very long time to come' – delivered as Labour's Attorney-General after the 1945 general election landslide victory, had such a powerful class content. That it was delivered when introducing legislation to parliament to extend trade union rights must have made it sound particularly threatening to Conservative ears. Labour in office was not labour in power, but the fact that the party which was either governing or forming the official opposition rested so squarely on the organised strength of trade unionism was a source of continuing concern to Britain's ruling elite.[7]

Initially, the establishment came to terms with this development. Given that the dominant leadership of the TUC and the major unions did not seek to challenge the existing social system and were more concerned to curb the class struggle than to use their strength to push it to any sort of a conclusion, there was no cause for panic. The prolonged post-war economic boom – that growth rates in Britain were highest when trade unions were strongest is an interesting fact of economic history that is very seldom taught – made the unions' investiture as an estate of the realm all the easier.[8]

Nevertheless, the years of union advance gave rise to a growing discontent in the establishment. Lord Donaldson, later Master of the Rolls, produced a pamphlet for the Conservative Party in the late 1950s advocating a reduction in union power by legislative means, but Harold MacMillan, busy as he was having it so good, never did anything about it. It was Labour, the union's own party but already enslaved to establishment ideas as to the 'national interest', which had the first crack at reining in working-class organisation by law with Barbara Castle's *In Place of Strife* proposals in 1969. The defeat of these by the unions, with some political help from within the government, was followed by Edward Heath's more determined and coercive legal attempts to bring the trade union movement to heel. This drew forth the biggest surge of trade union militancy since the General Strike of 1926, visiting one humiliation after another on the establishment. Heath's Industrial Relations Court (presided over by the same Donaldson) was defied, the hitherto obscure Official Solicitor had to be produced to release jailed dockers when their incarceration threatened to provoke a general strike, shipbuilding on the Clyde was saved following a prolonged sit-in and the miners' won two major confrontations with government in 1972 and 1974. The latter of these led Heath to call an election to give the public the chance to answer the question 'who runs the country?' The answer was along the lines of 'we're not really sure, but if you have to ask it certainly isn't you'.

What pushed Britain's rulers onto the path of confrontation with organised labour? The conventional argument is simply that Britain was in the grip of endless strikes, that union power was keeping productivity low and inhibiting economic growth and that, mainly through its historic connection with the Labour Party, the union movement had acquired political power that was excessive for a mere 'interest group' in a democracy. In fact, none of these arguments were better than half true. Outside the period of the Heath government, strikes were largely confined to a few industries, while labour's political power was insufficient to save the mainly Asian women workers at Grunwick from dismissal under a Labour government for demanding union recognition in 1976. However, these *canards* were widely believed and there were certainly people in both the leadership of the unions and in the working class more generally who internalised them, too.

Francis Williams, who surely expected the 'magnificent journey' to continue without end, still perhaps expressed a truth greater than he realised in 1954 when he noted that 'trade union development marches alongside that of modern capitalism.' The first underlying reason for the need to 'take on the unions' becoming more widely felt was exactly the changes in modern capitalism – the gradual exhaustion of the prolonged post-war economic expansion, which culminated in the collapse of the Bretton Woods currency exchange agreement in 1971 and the 'oil price shock' of 1973. These developments undermined the stability of world capitalism, put increasing pressure on profit rates and also raised the question of the continuing viability of the welfare state consensus which had prevailed in Britain, as elsewhere in Western

Europe, since 1945. None of these issues could be satisfactorily addressed within the framework of capitalism unless one sought the trade unions' co-operation in curbing living standards or, failing that, radically reduced their power.[9]

Some of these economic factors were common to all capitalist countries at the time. Yet the anti-union campaign assumed a unique virulence in Britain. This reflected more than just the particularly powerful position British unions had attained. Anglo-Saxon capitalism, dominated by the short-term considerations of financial returns to shareholders and the interests of the City, lacked the tradition of stable and long-term investment, not to mention management through social consensus, that emerged elsewhere in Europe after 1945. Britain, like the USA, suffers from a particular form of 'take-no-prisoners' capitalism under which the only restraining factor in pursuing the class war is the fear of defeat.

Beyond that, however, are other factors relating to ideology and class. The 1960s and 1970s were times of a great increase in working-class self-confidence in Britain. While the 1970s are now conventionally presented as some prolonged national disaster and the gloomiest of decades, that is not how they will be remembered by millions for whom they were a time of secure, relative prosperity. (The 1960s are condemned today too, on the grounds that they unleashed a permissive liberalism, but enhanced sexual opportunities, divorce and cannabis consumption have shown a cross-class appeal which collective working-class assertiveness lacks.) Employees were able to stand up for themselves at work, mass unemployment was a memory rather than a prospect, and the social ills which inevitably attend the systematic destruction of communities were as yet unimagined.

The great strike wave of the early 1970s did not merely have the result of maintaining or improving wage levels. In a number of celebrated cases 'workers' struggle and confrontations with the employers compelled the latter to negotiate over such areas as investment plans, and to permit manning problems to enter into the area of negotiations, making them subject to mutual agreement with then organised workers who thus achieved real decision-making'. In the first half of 1973 alone, fifty-seven sit-ins took place to prevent redundancies or closures, many of them successful. Employers were, in many cases, losing exclusive control over the work process itself, even where they retained ownership rights.[10]

The middle classes, or most of them, simply felt that the workers had got above themselves and that this was an unacceptable extension of working-class authority. Indeed the very phrase 'working class' became the butt of Conservative humour seeking to embed the idea that the British worker was by nature lazy when in actual fact workers were extending the real range of their activity in society as never before. The widely-popularised idea that 'managers have lost the right to manage' was more a call to mobilisation to reassert a faltering social hegemony than it was anything to do with promoting economic efficiency. Indeed, once given the 'right to manage' to their hearts' content, many British managers brought their industries to their knees.

And lurking behind all that was the fear of socialism. Over-heated Tory pundits claimed that Britain in the 1970s was already 'socialist', but wiser ruling-class heads knew that still worse could lie ahead. Mick McGahey, Vice-President of the National Union of Mineworkers, used to tell the story of his return to the family home as a young miner in 1947, excited after his first day working for the newly-nationalised coal industry. 'This is socialism', he said to his father, like

McGahey a Communist but one of an even more unyielding temper. 'Nationalisation is nae socialism,' the elder McGahey replied, 'socialism is working-class power.'

In the 1970s the Soviet Union, the socialist 'superpower', was a formidable counterweight to capitalism worldwide. No one could argue that there were no systemic alternatives to the freemarket system. The left, including Communist parties, was very strong in a number of countries of Western Europe. It appeared feasible to many, and not just to *Daily Mail* readers overcome by the vapours, that the trade unions, utilising their affiliation to the Labour Party, might be the agency through which bourgeois society would be brought to a peaceful end in Britain.

In fact, the trade unions neither had the intention – under 'moderate' leadership as they for the most part were – nor the capacity, as primarily economic organisations, of doing such a thing. For the great majority of trade unionists, including some left-wing leaders, the economic struggle was the end in itself. Challenging capitalist power structures would have required a *political* leap which was scarcely contemplated, let alone attempted.

Whatever mixture of rational and irrational motivations animated the establishment's thinking, there can be no doubt that following the humiliation of the miners' strike of 1974 and the 'three-day week', when the nation was enjoined to take baths in company in order to economise on heating, elements in the establishment started preparing their revenge in earnest.

There is no argument now that they were more successful than they no doubt dared hope at the time, it remains to consider why. First, despite the mystifying rhetoric about Britain becoming socialist in the 1970s, all the decisive instruments of economic and political power in Britain remained under capitalist control. Britain was a capitalist not a planned economy, based on private ownership. The courts, the police (including MI5 and Special Branch, whose anti-labour activities have only recently been coming to light) and, when the question came to be posed, the armed forces remained determinedly hostile to the labour movement. The resources that a government under reactionary leadership could bring to bear in an industrial confrontation were incomparably greater than could be mobilised by any one union, even the mightiest.

Second, the power of the trade unions could only be a factor if it were deployed. The years of the Wilson–Callaghan government from 1974 to 1979 saw the great mobilisations of earlier years dampened down. A centralised system of wage control – the 'social contract' – was developed which, in the name of defeating inflation, weakened collective bargaining, ultimately the foundation of trade union activity. Progressive social reforms were enacted by the government, but living standards were depressed, through real wage cuts, with the acquiescence of the TUC leadership. This had the consequence of fragmenting working-class solidarity to the point that in the end Callaghan was besieged both by the low paid in the famous 'winter of discontent' disputes and by the skilled engineering workers in the Midlands, who were feeling the squeeze of flat-rate pay rises, combined with inflation and diminishing tax thresholds, and wished to restore differentials.

Third, the sometimes exuberant militancy of the early 1970s was only unevenly reflected in a deeper political understanding. Winning higher wages through strike action does not of itself lead anyone to seek alternatives to the capitalist system. The view that 'things aren't working' became more widespread among trade union members themselves as the 1970s wore on and, in the absence of a clear lead towards an alternative perspective, the trade union movement lost considerable ideological ground to the Tories. Regional and craft differences remained to be exploited, as did still more profound racial and sexual divisions within the working class, issues the labour movement had barely begun to engage with in the 1970s. Many trade unionists also felt alienated from their own unions' structures – it is true that the Tory cure (legal interference in internal union business) was far worse than the complaint, but the existence of an underlying problem cannot be discounted.

The alliance between organised labour and progressive middle-class opinion, first consolidated in the 1930s and sustained ever since, also began to fall apart. The *Guardian* columnist Peter Jenkins developed his own critique of trade unionism in a book celebrating the launch of the Social Democratic Party, the right-wing (and anti-union) break-away from Labour initiated by David Owen, Roy Jenkins and Shirley Williams in 1981:

> The unions ... were unable to contribute effectively to growth strategies which depended upon wage restraint or improved productivity, partly because their antique structure and proce-dures were inadequate for the task, and partly because they could not exercise sufficient control over their members. The TUC ... had no effective authority over constituent unions; the unions, whose general secretaries ... were seldom wholly in control over their unions at district or shop-floor levels; district officers could do nothing with shop stewards, and even shop stewards were increasingly outflanked by rank-and-file militants. The more the unions became involved with government in

fixing wages, the more their members were inclined to see them as in collusion with employers. Most union leaders took it for granted that the unions' way of doing things was inevitable... Their attitude... contributed to the immobilisation of the trade union movement, it could neither reform itself nor be reformed, could satisfy its members neither by co-operating with governments nor by confronting them, and was unwilling and unable either to sustain the post-war order or to replace it with something better.[11]

Jenkins' critique from the right was based on the assumption that the deeper one went into the union ranks, the more militant the member you were likely to find, and that the failure of the unions was above all a failure to control this rank and file adequately. The trade-off which delivered wage restraint in return for programmes of moderate social reform was thereby broken.

Against this background, the Thatcher government, elected in the wake of the practical breakdown of relations between the unions and the Labour Party in the winter of 1978–79, set about its fundamental business of weakening organised labour. The struggle was fought on three fronts – the development of mass unemployment, the passage of laws which cumulatively reduced trade unionism to a state of semi-servitude without parallel in Western Europe and a series of set-piece confrontations with unions in different industries (always one at a time).

British industrial output fell by over 15 per cent in the early years of Mrs Thatcher's government, a slump without precedent in peace-time, and unemployment swelled to over three million (on official figures). This was a turn of events which not merely the trade unions but the country as a whole had imagined belonged as firmly to the past as sending children up chimneys. Most of those who lost their jobs were trade union members, since it was precisely the largely union-organised sectors of the economy like manufacturing which were hardest hit. The 'dole' returned as a way of life in working-class communities and the self-confidence and assertiveness of the preceding forty years turned to a mixture of anger and despair.

The leadership of most unions (and, let it be said, many senior Tories at the time) were simply bewildered that Thatcher and her Chancellor, Geoffrey Howe, did nothing to reflate the economy and act to avert the massive, and potentially dangerous, social dislocation which the return of mass unemployment was causing. While the Thatcherites justified their policy in terms of economic rationality, their motivation was equally political, explicitly aimed at a change in the balance of class power. This was the start of unemployment as being a 'price worth paying', in the celebrated words of a subsequent Tory Chancellor, to secure wider political (read class) objectives. Emboldened by the fact that the Tories got away with it politically, the post-war consensus that it was an object of government to promote full employment was noisily abandoned by a relieved establishment.

While the unions were lamenting an apparent return to the 1930s, Thatcher herself was busy ensuring that there would be no return to the 1970s and mass trade union resistance to Tory government policy. Piecemeal, a series of laws were introduced which would make any such possibility unlawful. Picketing was severely limited, and union–employer agreements requiring trade union membership as a condition of employment rendered illegal. Any action taken by workers in support of others was likewise placed beyond legal protection. Secret ballots were required before industrial action could be undertaken, rendering a swift response by employees to employer provocation impossible. Union funds were made liable to seizure if these provisions were not observed. As the decade wore on, legal interference in the internal conduct of union business was extended, mandating the form and conduct of union elections and prohibiting the exclusion of strike-breakers from unions, rulings which (unrepealed to this day) impose obligations on trade unions which no other voluntary organisation of citizens has to bear. The individual rights of employees were circumscribed to the point where the worker was virtually defenceless against employer abuse for the first two years of employment, and it was ruled lawful for a company to discriminate against an individual on the grounds of his or her trade union membership. Many of these laws placed Britain in breach of its obligations under International Labour Organisation conventions.

This tirade of legislation was all opposed, of course, by the TUC. However, there was no return to the mass defiance of the law of ten years earlier. Right from the start, some union leaders were signalling a retreat before the offensive, although there was also a weak spirit of opposition amongst the union membership as a whole. The AUEW, then the country's second-largest union, had returned to a right-wing position following the retirement of Hugh Scanlon as its President. The formidable alliance of the TGWU and the AUEW, which had been at the heart of the resistance to Heath, was no more. The AUEW's General Secretary, Sir John Boyd, signalled submission as early as 1980 when he said 'we are not looking for conflict and we do not think there is any need for it. We are not advising our members to break the law of the land.'[12] The leaders of the electricians' union, the EETPU, were still more prepared to accommodate the Thatcher legal agenda. Both unions became more agitated about opposing the left-wing and anti-nuclear weapons activists in the Labour Party than about resisting their union's own loss of its ability to conduct many essential activities lawfully. The role of state interference in the trade unions and the corruption of individual leaders may have played a larger part in these developments than we have yet been told.

The record of the 1980s is of one trade union after another fighting – and losing – in isolation. Every proud union took strike action or was locked out – invariably, they were defensive battles, seeking to preserve jobs or long-honoured conditions of service – and each now must record a more-or-less disastrous defeat in its history.

The train drivers had the 'flexible rostering' dispute of 1982 in an attempt to preserve the guaranteed eight-hour day, in place for sixty years; the printers had first Eddie Shah's Warrington operation and then News International's move to Wapping, when Rupert Murdoch eliminated five thousand jobs overnight; the seafarers had the P&O dispute; television workers had TV-AM; the dockers lost the national dock labour scheme, their guarantee against the insecurity of casual employment for two generations, in 1989.

And, of course, there was the great miners' strike of 1984–85, for which Thatcher had made the most detailed and meticulous preparation. There was to be no repeat of 1974 – the miners and their union were punished for their earlier victories. The government's tactics included spying on and splitting the NUM and the deployment of a variety of police methods which ranged from wholesale breach of the right to free movement to kidnap and torture.[13] Thatcher won: the pits were closed as Arthur Scargill had predicted and today there is an epidemic of heroin addiction gripping communities where coal was once mined.

Almost as bad as that outcome, however, has been the systematic subsequent criticism of the miners' struggle by the leadership of the labour movement, leaving their endurance dishonoured in defeat by the condescending contempt of 'progressive' opinion. It is routine to hear Scargill blamed for the pit closure programme, as if Mrs Thatcher had not planned it with precision, to hear the miners dubbed as donkeys for trying to preserve their communities and livelihoods against a menace which was abundantly real and which has since been more comprehensively consummated than anyone envisaged, to hear the NUM reproved for failing to grasp economic realities, although the destruction of the mining industry was a political project from start to finish, designed to rip the heart out of any class-conscious labour organisation in Britain. This rewriting of recent history within the labour movement has one practical objective above all – it is to engrave *Never Again* on the hearts and minds of a generation.

No doubt this has been in some measure successful. At the bitter conclusion of every strike some on the left could be found to say 'the fightback starts now'. It didn't. It is easy to underestimate what a traumatic experience taking industrial action of that duration, and in such an environment of bitterness, is and how painfully defeat can be felt. It can make the individuals concerned at best reluctant to repeat the exercise in their own lifetime, even if they are in a position to contemplate it and their jobs are not lost for good. It can do worse – it can destroy the cohesion of communities, particularly where employment and residence closely intertwine, and even of families as children see their parents defeated and humiliated. The scars of industrial defeat bite deep, and are slow to heal. It took the 1939–45 war to set the trade union movement fully back on its feet after the defeat of the General Strike. Some argue that Britain's miners only finally laid the ghosts of 1926 to rest in 1972.

And the setbacks in the struggles of the 1980s had an additional twist to them, absent in previous such episodes in the twentieth century – the closures and cutbacks which attended them were, or certainly looked to be, permanent. The mines, shipyards, steel works and factories which had been shut down were never to be re-opened, unless it be under a government so radically different as to be beyond the political imagination of the labour movement's leadership of the time. This was not the consequence of a routine cyclical downturn, but of a seismic shift in Britain's place in the world economy. With it, the entire culture formed through two centuries of industrial development was shaken as never before.

Other political factors also shaped the conditions which brought the 'magnificent journey' to a halt. Labour lost the 1983 general election heavily, fighting on a radical manifesto which had job creation at its core. This manifesto was immediately dubbed 'the longest suicide note in history' by Gerald Kaufman, with his facility for the glib and misleading phrase. The view that Labour lost because it was too left-wing became unchallengeable wisdom.

Yet three factors contributed to that defeat which vastly magnified its margin: the Falklands War and the chauvinism it aroused; the decision of an illustrious group of Labour right-wingers to break away from the Party and found the SDP, with considerable media support; and the fact that Michael Foot was unable to unite Labour or present himself as an attractive option as Prime Minister. Of course, the last two factors could be seen as consequences of Labour's leftwards move, and of misjudged tactics by those who inspired that shift, but the policies themselves made neither inevitable. While it might strain credibility to say that Labour could have won in 1983 on its radical platform, the scale of the electoral catastrophe was surely not down to policies which, taken on their own, attracted considerable opinion poll support.

The defeat of 1983 was repeated four years later, but, in an early example of self-interested spinning, Labour's communications manager in 1987, Peter Mandelson, ensured that the campaign would be seen as a triumph on account of the production of a modern, personality-driven party political broadcast featuring Neil Kinnock. The media loved it, even though the result showed voters unmoved. It was after 1987 that the 'modernising' project really got under way in the Labour Party with the unions, for the first time, being seen as an embarrassing liability.

The political malaise was deepened by other developments. The Communist Party, the school in which generations of working-class leaders, from the shopfloor to the union leaderships, had been trained, collapsed in a prolonged internecine struggle. Even as developments in the economy were undermining the Party's industrial roots, the 'Eurocommunist' leadership began expelling its left-wing critics, including many of the Party's best-known union figures, from the mid-1980s onwards. This argument consumed vast amounts of the time and energy of people who the broader working-class movement could not really spare for such feuding. The split was nourished by, and in turn fed, the disintegration of the wider left, which had long looked, directly or indirectly, to the Communist Party for ideological and strategic guidance. It is only recently that the Party has started to recover some of this influence.

International events played a part, too. The degeneration of Mikhail Gorbachev's *perestroika* into the restoration of capitalism in the Soviet Union, and the overturning of the socialist system in Eastern Europe in the late 1980s, further undermined the view that public ownership of the economy provided a viable alternative to the free-market triumphalism, trumpeted long and loud by Mrs Thatcher and Ronald

Reagan. The Soviet Union had not been seen as a model for Britain's own development by very many within the trade union movement for years, but the idea that it offered definite social advantages compared to capitalism and, with internal reform, could offer still more, was fairly deep-rooted. At the very least, the rhetoric of egalitarianism offered a global counter-point to the celebration of privilege; just as the very existence of the Soviet Union had placed certain (if diminishing) restraints on the internal behaviour of ruling classes throughout Europe. The International Labour Organisation, for example, was established after the First World War in large part to offer labour an alternative to Bolshevism, and the creation of the welfare state can be seen as the tribute paid by capitalism to Communism.

So the 'end of history' bit deep into the depleting political reserves of the British labour movement. I recall one discussion with T&G General Secretary Bill Morris about the demand for public ownership of something or other in the early 1990s, which ended with him inquiring 'since the Soviet Union's gone, what does public ownership or socialism mean now anyway?' He was being genuinely quizzical, not polemical. Such uncertainty was widespread. The T&G and most other Labour-affiliated unions opposed Tony Blair's move to rewrite the historic Clause Four of the Party's constitution, which notionally committed the Party to common ownership of the means of production, in 1995, but their opposition lacked passion and conviction. Ten years earlier, however, it was impossible to imagine Labour's right-wing even embarking on such an argument, much less winning it. The intervening demise of the Soviet experience was the difference.

3

Looking Back and Looking Ahead – Jack Jones and Ken Gill

Jack Jones

Fighting is a word that looms large in conversation with Jack Jones about the trade union movement – fighting unions, fighting workers, a fighting unity. Few ninety-year-olds are so pugnacious.

But then fighting is what Jack Jones has done throughout his life – as a volunteer in the war against fascism in Spain, as a trade union organiser in the Midlands, as a national official and ultimately General Secretary of the T&G. Fighting for democracy, for decent employment and living conditions for the working class and for equality.

The press in the 1970s had Jack Jones down as the 'most powerful man in the country', outranking prime ministers and all. Statement of fact or flattery, it certainly never went to his head. Since retiring as T&G leader a quarter of a century ago, he has dedicated himself to fighting for a better deal for Britain's pensioners.

Unglamorous work, but for those for whom to live is to fight, it gives a focus and a purpose. It has also allowed him to visit a modest office in successive

Transport Houses, the home of the T&G, several times a week. The T&G is still in his blood. When he says 'we' he means the union he served, when he says 'they' he is most often referring to the people who lead it now.

Do you see signs of a revival in the trade union movement today?
The election of a new general secretary at amicus [*Derek Simpson*] is tremendous news. If he has the driving force to make real changes, then that is the most heartening news that I have heard recently. I am sure there will be a lot of goodwill towards him in the AEU branches in particular.

But if we are to have a real revival, the major thing that is essential is an effective shop stewards movement. The trade union movement at the base is not sufficiently strong and militant. It is still the basis for developing strategies. We have got to start building the unions back into the districts. We used to have two hundred district offices, it is down to sixty today. It is not going to be easy, but we have got to make a start – get the unions back closer to the factories and rebuild the shop stewards movement. It's one of the areas the left of the movement should be looking at. General secretaries think that they are the cat's whiskers, but if you pay attention to the localities, there is the possibility of achieving victories.

At the end of your memoirs, nearly twenty years ago, you say that the main issues facing the trade unions are dealing with multinational companies and technological change. How do you think we've done?
We've talked about Europe a lot, but we've not built strong European links of a fighting character. You have trade union people, officials going abroad the whole time, but it's like a holiday: over in Europe

every five minutes, but not really representing working people – it's an exchange of views between officials removed from the workshop.

Finding people from the rank and file, building those links and that relationship would be important. There's no problem having international committees, but we're not working at building a fighting trade union internationalism. And we've not really tackled technological change either – we have a very weak international trade union movement. There's no punch there, although the International Transport Workers Federation – that's one that still has meaning, still tries to battle.

Well, it's twenty years on now, why do you think we haven't got further?
The spirit was hounded out of us by Thatcherism, quite deliberately so. And we reacted in a rather constitutional way. I don't really want to criticise but Ron [*Todd, T&G General Secretary 1985–92*] was wrong when the National Dock Labour scheme was abolished. It should have been challenged straightaway by strike action, because that was something of strategic value that we had. Now we've lost the docks membership. We lost the one area where we could organise solidarity action.

The law made it difficult …
The law has always been against us.

Could a different policy have been followed?
Thinking about what might have been is the biggest waste of time. But today the unions do not seem to be pressing as much as they should be. The government can be made to give way, we can take those opportunities. But the solidarity amongst unions is not as great as it should be. Simpson must be cultivated, he can be a good friend.

The quote of yours cited most often today is the one about the union–Labour link – murder yes, divorce never ...

Murder many times ... the trade union movement would be very foolish to allow a break, although it may satisfy Blair. For the working class to have any possibility of political influence it must be on a major political party, and we should exercise it as strongly as we can. It's just that some of the people we send to Labour committees don't do it.

Frank Cousins used to say let's have a trade union party. But working people won't vote for a trade union party. It would be impossible to create a new large-scale party. Of course you can have small parties with correct policies, but the trade unions need to have influence on a major party. They should be more assertive – my feeling is that the trade union leaders should be more socialistically inclined, as we were in the past. You have got to see the political party and the unions as part of a common fight to improve the lot of the working classes, and you have to send people into the Party who are fighters.

I suppose something has gone wrong. Not so many people link trade unions with a socialist outlook. Union education has become divorced from the political angle. Trade unions cannot exist without political action.

There are many people today in the trade union movement who have divorced themselves from any convictions. They fell into the trap of wanting big cars, big houses and living the lives of the ultra-rich. They have got this idea that because they are trade union leaders they deserve a big car and a big house. You should live as trade unionists live. That is what I have always done. It's not any sense of superiority, it's just the way it should be.

Perhaps the temptations are greater now.

The temptations were always there. The boss says come to a game of golf, come to lunch and in the end the trade union official becomes an arm of the industrial relations department.

There's a huge organising job to be done if the unions are to get back to where they were in the 1970s.
It won't be as easy as all that. The workforce is in smaller units now. That is why you have got to base the union as it was, in the localities, in the districts. Morris and company think all you need is a car and a telephone. They should reduce finance here [*JJ gestures at Transport House around him*]. You have got to recruit more district officers, to keep in touch, and follow through on new plans.

What about union services, financial offers and so on?
Biggest waste of money ever by unions. You do not recruit or consolidate on that basis at all.

So, are you hopeful?
There is a growing awareness of the need for change. But we remain over-developed here [*Transport House*] without enough at the bottom. You can see the demands in the localities. There is still a militant movement, still a desire to organise, but it needs support and inspiration from the centre, which is not forthcoming. Trade unionism has to be based on the strength of character of your activists in the localities, in the place of work. We don't want to make them better business operators, but better activists and agitators.

How do you feel about social partnership?
It's terrible. It's an idea that should never have got off the ground – it was an alternative to being more militant. Of course, employers

were always mouthing it. Had we had stronger leadership here, build-ing up more militancy, we could have been more effective in the field.

What has happened in many of our industries is that we have management-dominated payment systems, without any worker involve-ment. This has weakened efforts to build up trade unionism, and weakened them where they already operated. We have lost control of payment systems. Unions like the T&G, GMB, MSF all fell for it. The ETU were architects of it. The acme of the system was the partner-ship between the ETU and the bosses in actually controlling the men.

Workers have got to be assisted to fight, encouraged to fight in some circumstances. The T&G and the AEU together – that would be a good thing, that would disarm the right. I think the average local officer would respond to stronger leadership. It can't be achieved overnight, but we are starting to see some strength in the trade union movement again. It will take time to get confidence back in the labour force, the confidence to stand up together.

You don't get it from TUC documents – all those resolutions that mean nothing, lead to nothing.

Ken Gill

Ken Gill dismisses rhetoric (espoused in a television programme by Arthur Scargill a day or two before our interview) that presents trade union campaigns as surrogate revolutionary movements. It is a view that carries particular weight because Gill is himself a revolutionary – a life-long member of the Communist Party who rose to the very top of the trade union movement as the General Secretary of the white-collar engineering union TASS and, after a merger with ASTMS, MSF. He also served on the TUC General Council throughout the years of Labour's late 1970s

political collapse and the subsequent Thatcher disasters – he was to all practical pur-
poses the leader of the left on the General Council throughout that traumatic period.

Talk about trade unions bringing down the government is hopeless. Of course, you can oppose a government policy, and if as a by-product that brings them down, then that's fine. But saying your aim is to overthrow the government is the death-knell for whatever cause you're fighting for.

There were moments when the left was almost winning votes in the General Council – when Murdoch was taking the work away from Fleet Street to Wapping, when we could have had real solidarity action and given actual support to the unions concerned.

The left was influenced by the [*Communist*] Party and it is important to say so now. The Party, when it was operating under Bert Ramelson [*CP industrial organiser 1965–77*] used to put its propositions into the left, but it did not stand or die by them. It was flexible, it had an input but did not fight for the line regardless.

The decline of the Communist Party affected the left, no doubt about it at all. Rodney Bickerstaffe used to say 'when is the Party going to make itself clear'. It was very difficult because the Party was practically disowning me on every occasion then.

Eric Hobsbawm's autobiography is just out. He obviously feels he was vindicated
on the whole 'Forward March of Labour halted' argument, of which you were one
of the main protagonists, on the other side, in the late 1970s ...
Well, he has been vindicated. I was saying that we would have a growing militancy in the trade union movement and that it would re-establish its central role. I said it because I believed it, but it was not so.

A lot of the old Eurocommunists are writing very critical articles now. They spent the 1980s fighting against the Soviet Union and the traditional left and labour movement in Britain. One's gone and the other's weakened and they do not like the world that we are left with.

I welcome the fact that they are writing what they write. It is significant. I would like to have asked Hobsbawm what he feels about the end of the Soviet Union. I feel that somehow or other the left has to re-invent the Soviet Union, obviously not reproduce what happened, but to put it in a really positive historical light. I do not think the struggle for socialism will really take off again until the Soviet Union is seen, for all its problems, as a huge step forward for working people in the world.

So why did the forward march of labour stop when it did?
Unemployment was the main weapon that destroyed the confidence and the ability of the trade unions to do anything. If we had had full employment, the working class would have resisted, despite the ideological attacks.

I was sent as an organiser to Liverpool in the early 1960s. It was considered a graveyard for officials then, so the right-wing in the union sent me up there to fail. This was when Ford was just moving into Merseyside, and it was grim there, no fight. But when people got jobs, suddenly militancy became a Liverpool characteristic, and there was a revival in a town which had really been discarded by capitalism.

I had never seen anything like it. Really, what happened there made me General Secretary of the union. We were successful in recreating a fighting spirit among people who had been terrified, and were doffing caps to employers. I had been told by my predecessors that you could not do anything with the workers in Liverpool. But then we had General Motors, AC Delco and others coming in and there were jobs everywhere. When people got sacked, they just got another job. It was great to know that if you went on strike and a factory shut down, you could just get work somewhere else. It was the unemployment of 1980 to 1983 that was the major attack on the movement, it was a conscious tool. After that came the [*anti-union*] measures.

People go on about the 1970s being a terrible time, but they were a great period for the working class. It was a marvellous time for working people, and also the source of much of the best social legislation.

I remember Billy Hayes saying how great the 1960s were – you had The Beatles, Keynesianism and that at the end of the 1960s almost everyone in Liverpool was living in a better house.
There you are then. People were not unhappy. You didn't have the jails full then.

In the 1970s, at Automatic Telephones if someone came in with a clipboard and a pencil, everyone would stop, they would not accept any time-and-motion arrangements. The company offered me a Rolls Royce if I could persuade the workers to co-operate. The manager said to me: 'Just think what we could do with this firm if they would co-operate. What would it take to get you to help persuade them?' I said, 'Well, a Rolls Royce might do ...' The manager said, 'All right then', and I had to say, 'No. For God's sake, I was just pulling your leg!'

The left came naturally then. People's ambitions were fed by the desire for a better life. I am not certain why trade unionists are voting for left leaders now. It must be that they are just fed up with all the things that are imposed on them at work and all the working practices, and they are fed up with it being presented [*by their unions*] as some kind of special partnership, when in fact they are just being bullied.

One of the trends in recent years has been for trade union leaders to mimic management in terms of the money they pay themselves and people are bound to say why are we paying this money and they are operating on behalf of management.

One of the weaknesses has always been this lack of theory in the British labour movement, a concentration on militancy without socialism.

Almost a contempt for theory. It is one of our weaknesses as compared to other European countries. Their social democracy has not collapsed to the same really humiliating extent as ours. They have hung on to their advances, important things like holidays, pensions, all the things that make your life a broader one, not only wages. People here do not know what you are talking about if you mention the social wage. It makes you vulnerable to counter-attack if you do not understand that winning all these things from the capitalist class is part of the class struggle.

Do you see a revival in the movement now?

It is much more tenuous than the media suggest. Very fragile. It's bound to be. You have a Labour government which is more reactionary than any Tory government, with the possible exception of Mrs Thatcher's. It confuses people.

And unemployment still exists in parts of the country – the parts that produced many of our best people in the past – the north-west, north-east, where heavy industry was. There is still very large unemployment there. And the psychology created by mass unemployment is still there – it lingers on long after the fact of unemployment has gone.

It's most important that the T&G gets a good leadership. The election of Derek Simpson was significant. I don't know him, I don't know how tough he is, but at the moment he is sounding all right. There's tremendous pressure on him to accommodate, but he's not doing that, and nor is he going off his rocker, as some people would like to see him do. I would say that the defeat of New Labour is the important thing. It causes massive confusion.

Blair says – and a lot of people believe him – that the only alternative to his government is a Tory one, that there is no left-wing alternative.
The Tories have been destroyed by New Labour. That really states the obvious. It is because the Tories have had their policies robbed by New Labour that it is only left with an eccentric right-wing to represent. The Labour Party is firmly established where the Tories once where. We have got to point out that this is a Tory Labour Party, but that there is sufficient history and sufficient institutions left to change it.

Some want to break that link …
It is a dangerous situation. And people should not kid themselves about Gordon Brown. A lot of people say he has a good relationship with the labour movement, but he is an ideologue deeply embedded in American-style capitalism. Belief in Brown is an illusion.

If you cannot win back the Party you've subsidised for socialism of some kind, then you are certainly not going to be able to start another mass party. But I would not say that we could go on [*supporting Labour*] regardless, regardless, regardless. But unless unions have an involvement with any challenge you are not going to get anywhere.

Union organisation needs strengthening, too.
I would have said that employment levels today should be conducive to

trade unionism. But people will only come back if they think there is power in the unions. The recent history, when trade unions have become sort of discount societies, and at work offering partnership with no hope of equality, why would anyone want to join that. They would be able to look after themselves without paying a subscription to a union.

There is enormous scope in private industry – organising has always been relatively easy in the public services, where there is more of a tradition of tolerance. I remember times in my life when we could not cope with the influx of members wanting to join, but then when unemployment hit us, the bleeding became unstoppable, and organising and recruiting was just alien to most union officials, they just did not want to go out and organise.

If you get into a fight and you win some sort of a victory, that helps consolidate membership. Tactical leadership is very important – making sure you can get some sort of a victory. We used to do that well in TASS, people always felt that something had been achieved as a result of a struggle.

The internationalisation of money and power has been much more rapid in recent times. When we were trying to extend the concept of international solidarity to our members in the 1960s and 1970s, the capitalist class was not moving much faster than us. Now the globalisation process, the undermining of the sovereign state has gone much further. We should promote the idea of sovereignty, running our own affairs, and letting other countries manage their own affairs.

The organisational base of trade unions has changed considerably. There was a tendency to reflect craft, but that reflected the organisation of the employers, it reflected the system of ownership. Now ownership is so spread, you need bigger mass organisations, with special interest groups to look after particular areas. Unions like the T&G have a modern structure. But in big private industry, our organisations are not always suitable.

I was talking to Jack Jones – he would probably agree that the T&G way is the right one.

Well, there's a tradition there. It was always said that Ernie Bevin regarded even the Soviet Union as a breakaway from the T&G.

4

Social Partnership and Europe

B y the start of the 1990s, the trade union movement was in a position changed out of all recognition, one which would have
seemed unbelievable had it been presented in the 1970s as the likely
future. Its collective membership was heading downwards towards
seven million, a figure passed on the ascent fifty years earlier, and its
base in the private sector was shrinking rapidly, as old, organised
industries cut back or disappeared altogether and new ones proved
resistant to efforts to organise. The unions seemed politically margin-
alised, doomed to chafe indefinitely under legal restraints unthinkable
elsewhere in Europe and bereft of even such clarity of purpose that
the nostrums of 'old Labourism' had provided.

The leadership of the movement pinned its hopes of a revival
throughout the 1990s on three main pillars – embrace of the
European Union, social partnership with employers, and acquiescence in the development of New Labour as an electoral necessity to
displace the Tories. These have dominated the story of union politics
for the last decade, and it is this strategy, which never quite reached
the point of consensus to begin with, which is now being challenged

by the rise of a revived left within the unions and by the first signs of a new rank-and-file assertiveness.

Trade unions had traditionally been broadly 'eurosceptic', and had nearly-unanimously been on the 'no' side in the 1975 referendum on Common Market entry. Their hostility was based on well-founded fears that the development of a single market in Europe would expose the jobs of many workers to a competition in which, given the historic poverty of investment in British industry, they would be the losers, and on the view that the development of a supra-national economic authority working in the interests of private capital, as codified in the EEC's rules, would block the expected evolution of British society towards some form of socialism. The start of a wholesale change in attitude was the loss of the general election in 1983 by Labour, a defeat which some attributed in part to scare stories that the policy of withdrawal from the EEC would itself cost jobs.

The change picked up pace, however, when the Brussels commission under French socialist Jacques Delors started to develop a 'social dimension' to the EU's agenda, hitherto seen as almost entirely pro-business. This produced fresh perceptions on both sides of the political divide in Britain. Tories who had hitherto seen the EU as a barrier to domestic development towards socialism (which they no longer much feared in any case) now began to see it as an agency which might roll back the 'freedom for business and enterprise' enshrined by Thatcher (who set no store at all by any social amelioration through law). On the other hand, the unions now felt that it might open a continental route to social reforms and tripartite consultations in industry, the Tories having blocked the domestic one. The visit of Delors to address the 1989 TUC congress and the warm reception he received for an address which was as critical of the

British government's social policy as diplomacy permitted, represented the flowering of this strategy. Its essence has been expressed by TUC General Secretary John Monks in the post-socialist formula that Britain now faces a choice between US-style capitalism and EU-style capitalism, and that the latter is clearly preferable for trade unionists.

The argument over this issue gathered force through the 1990s within the trade unions, as within society more generally. The controversies over the Maastricht Treaty and the development of the Euro, the EU's common currency, are mainly noted for the near-paralysing divisions which they have caused within the Conservative Party. The unions and, by extension, the Labour Party have, however, embraced an equally-wide range of views. The draconian government spending and budget criteria laid down in the Maastricht Treaty seemed to threaten the funding of public services, and hence workers within them, above all. Already battered by more than a decade of Tory neglect, it is unsurprising that public service workers have been the most resistant to the extension of the European project. Unison, the largest union in the public services, is opposed to the Euro.

The terms of the argument have been different in industry, where Britain's isolation in the single market and, thereafter, the single currency, has been seen as a threat to inward investment and, hence, jobs. Yet in this sector, while the AEU was a crusader for British entry into the Euro (at least until the downfall of Sir Ken Jackson), the T&G has been considerably cooler. The TUC itself has been the most unabashed advocate of all things EU. It has argued that the institutions of the Union could impose social decency on hostile British governments and employers, and that the continental model of 'social partnership' – three-way negotiation of social and economic issues between employers, unions and government – could be imported into

Britain, at the expense of Thatcherite confrontation, via the agency of EU initiatives.

The terms of this argument have started to shift against the pro-EU position. First, the EU commands tiny resources compared with those available to the nation-state, so it would be unable to fund any serious efforts at social amelioration in the first place. Second, the TUC has embraced the European 'social model' just as the latter is looking more than frayed at the edges. The introduction of the Euro has been accompanied by an intensifying budget squeeze across Europe, and mounting pressure both to cut back the welfare state and dismantle some of the entrenched social gains made by trade unions in earlier years. Under pressure of globalisation, Monks' two 'models' of capitalism are showing increasing signs of convergence. Third, unemployment remains extremely high in most countries in the 'Euro-zone', which undermines the jobs argument to a significant degree. And fourth, the British Labour government has itself emerged as a leader of those seeking to *diminish* the EU's 'social dimension' and block any further pro-labour reforms, like equal rights for temporary and part-time workers and legal limitations on working time. The new leader of amicus, Derek Simpson, has cited one example of the effects of this: 'When the CBI opposes a compulsory [EU] directive on equal pay, the government makes it voluntary. And, predictably, only 300 businesses are implementing it. There is an 18% pay gap and at the rate of change since the Equal Pay Act was passed, it will be 40 years before we get equal pay.'[14]

The second, and related, leg of the 1990s strategy has not fared any better. 'Social partnership' has proved a disappointment by any measure. There is scope for argument about how much this idea is entirely new. If it means simply the process of trade unions coming to an agreement with an employer which both sides hope will be mutually beneficial, or at least they can both live with, then it is nothing more than a different label for what has been the enduring business of industrial relations. However, its advocates (almost all on the union side of the table, which should have been an early warning sign) have made more exalted claims on its behalf. 'We are prepared to discuss flexibility, and changes in the way we work, to make British companies competitive in return for the job security which is valued above all else ... Our mission at the T&G is to work hand-in-hand with employers to build a modern, productive, competitive economy in the interests of the nation, its industries and its people', Bill Morris said in 1996.[15]

The most immediate difficulty with the partnership model is that it is one of those relationships where three is not only not a crowd, but the bare minimum needed to get going. Absent government involvement in the process (as opposed to mumbled good-will from a distance), there is no possibility of the partnership being one of equals. New Labour has shown not the slightest desire to reverse the Thatcher–Major distaste for any such involvement. Neither at a strategic nor at a sectoral level has it done anything to engage with employers and unions on a tripartite basis, with the exception of training questions. Anxious to avoid Conservative accusations of a return to 1970s-style 'corporatism', it has done little more than demand that the two remaining social partners get along with each other. This on its own would leave unchecked the fundamental imbalance in power between employers and employees, something even Peter Mandelson has acknowledged. That imbalance is worsened, however, by the government taking almost every chance to display its preference for the outlook and demands of business.

The power inequality has been brutally displayed throughout the 1990s. The core problem with social partnership is not a matter of cynical bosses swindling gullible union representatives, although no doubt there are any number of employers who might like to try. Rather, it is a necessarily vain attempt to suspend the operation of the basic laws of capitalism.

The most important of these, which exists quite independently of the will or opinions of any particular capitalist, is the search for the maximum possible profit. This drives capital accumulation in whatever specific context a company or industry operates.

The broad context today includes radically reduced restrictions on the free movement of capital, the internationalisation of the production of many commodities and a range of coercive measures to maintain a vast supply of cheap labour in many parts of the world.

Thus management may think it means it when it tells the trade unions that, if the workers will only produce more goods faster and cheaper, their jobs will be guaranteed. But what are those words worth when a competitor finds they can slash production costs and grab market share by establishing a factory on a broadly comparable technical basis, but only by employing labour at a tenth of the cost, in another country – in Eastern Europe or the Far East?

There is no capitalist, however liberal, honourable or god-fearing, who will fall on an economic sword for the sake of keeping an agreement with trade unions. Times have changed, as Ford of Europe boss Nick Scheele told trade unions when he explained the company's decision to go back on its commitment, made just three years previously, to maintain car assembly at the Dagenham plant. He has since been promoted by Ford, while thousands of workers in East London have been laid off, an eloquent enough commentary on the content of social partnership and the value of an employer's pledge.

Such examples could be multiplied. The textile industry has been decimated. A union commitment to partnership has not saved Britain's steel plants from massive cutbacks. 'Newer' industries like financial services have also seen massive job losses. In fact, almost all the companies highlighted as model social partners by the TUC just three years ago have declared thousands of redundancies since.

To take perhaps the most celebrated example, again from the motor industry: the first social partnership agreement heralded as such by the T&G was with Rover. In return for new working practices which were so unpopular that the workforce only narrowly assented to them, the company promised in the early 1990s to guarantee employment and avoid redundancies. This 'partnership' held good for no more than a few years before the company's owners, BMW, made swingeing job cuts and in 2000 the company's main plant, at Longbridge in Birmingham, was faced with total shutdown. The loss of tens of thousands of jobs, directly or indirectly, was averted not by 'social partnership' but by a high-profile campaign led by the T&G's Tony Woodley and involving the wider Midlands community.

In essence, social partnership has helped big companies raise the rate of exploitation of their workforce, by getting fewer workers to produce more for no corresponding increase in wages, yet has proved utterly powerless when it comes to defending jobs. It could not be otherwise – the very rhetoric which usually accompanies partnership deals, the talk of uniting to 'beat the competition', gives the clue. In any competition there are winners as well as losers, so even in a TUC 'best case' scenario, of social partnership everywhere, many workers would find the fruits of the trade-off bitter indeed.

It is therefore small surprise that Derek Simpson wrote in his election literature that:

> Partnership is a sop, developed on the back of an appeal to our basic instinct that we can get something for nothing. In truth what we are being drawn into is quite the opposite. It is about us getting nothing for something! By undermining collective bargaining by the partnership approach we are opening ourselves to wide scale exploitation without the means to secure adequate recompense and the little job security that appears to exist rapidly disappears as soon as the bosses find greener pastures.[16]

The success of this message in a union which has gone further than any other in promoting the 'partnership approach' is the most vivid expression of working-class frustration with it.

5

Challenging New Labour

I happened to be in the company of two senior union leaders on the night John Smith died. One was particularly, and understandably, morose. In the end he observed 'now it will be Brown or Blair and you can't trust either of them'.

The issue of whether it was to be Brown or Blair was famously being settled by New Labour's ruling duo at Granita, a restaurant in Islington. At the time nobody entertained the now-fashionable folly that there is a significant political difference between the two. And nobody in the union leaderships, with the exception of Sir Ken Jackson, never knowingly outflanked on the right, wanted either of them. The rank and file, however, in unions and Party alike, were swept up in media enthusiasm for the telegenic Mr Blair whose election as leader was therefore, *inter alia*, presented as yet another rebuke to the union hierarchy by the membership.

Under these circumstances, once their protests at the off-hand abolition of the commitment to common ownership had been swept aside, most unions decided to go along with the new dispensation in the Party – one which was committed to putting to the sword everything trade unionism held dear. So great was the desire to see an end to the Tories' unprecedented run of electoral victories that the big unions bore with forebearance the endless humiliations visited on them between 1994 and 1997 by Blair and his coterie of increasingly insolent spin-doctors. Journalists who witnessed the scene still remark on the ill-mannered way in which Blair greeted Bill Morris when arriving to address the T&G's conference in 1995. That he was invited at all was a testimony to Morris's powers of forgiveness, since earlier in the year Blair had worked might and main to replace the T&G General Secretary, Britain's first black trade union leader, with Jack Dromey, whose campaign theme was 'New Labour, New T&G'.

The fact that Morris prevailed in that bitterly-contested and high-profile election with unexpected ease, despite it being held at New Labour's flood-tide, was a first sign that while union members might be happy for Blair to lead the Labour Party, they did not want him running their unions by proxy.

Blair himself came to the TUC Congress in 1997 in the wake of Labour's first election victory to deliver a stinging and contemptuous rebuke to those who had been Labour's strongest supporters throughout its eighteen years in opposition. I will be watching your behaviour, he said. No-one dared tell him that it is not the business of the elected to scrutinise his electors, but rather the reverse.

However stunted the expectations the unions still entertained of New Labour in 1997, they have still not been fulfilled. It is this which provides much of the indispensable context to the recent revival of the left and of trade union militancy.

The dwindling coterie of Blair–Brown enthusiasts still assert that trade unionists have much to be grateful for: a minimum wage has been introduced, although at a considerably lower rate than the movement desired and that social justice required, with an even lower rate for young workers; a law has been introduced making trade union recognition easier to obtain, and extending some rights at work for individuals, including issues like parental leave; the Tory 'opt out' of EU social legislation has been abandoned and replaced by a determination to obstruct the adoption of any further significant social measures at EU level instead; and you have to wait eight weeks before you are allowed to sack strikers. But the great majority of restrictive legislation passed between 1979 and 1997 remains on the statute book.

With the single crisis-driven exception of the bankrupt Railtrack, no privatisation has been reversed. On the contrary, air traffic control has been sold off, with disastrous consequences; the London Underground has been entwined in a fiendishly complex and wildly unpopular 'private–public partnership' scheme which seems to serve no purpose beyond the enrichment of construction companies; the controversial Private Finance Initiative projects have been radically extended; and Blair has now promised the further introduction of privatisation into the health, education and local government services. Not only does this strike at the heart of some of the cherished achievements of post-war social democracy, it threatens to create a two-tier workforce, with those transferred to the private sector progressively seeing their pay and conditions driven relatively downwards. While union pressure at the height of the government's difficulties with the FBU and over Iraq secured an agreement designed to limit this, it must be doubted whether it will withstand the pressure of private sector economic realities for long.

Social inequality has, for the first time ever under a Labour government, been widened rather than narrowed. As the *Guardian*'s Economics Editor wrote:

the explosion of top pay has made Britain a more unequal society than it has ever been. The gap between rich and poor has widened under Labour, entirely because the already rich have become stupendously richer ... Britain is on course to end two terms of a Labour government with a greater degree of inequality than it had after 18 years of the Conservatives. Not something for a social democratic party to be proud of.[17]

But this is not social democracy as we know it. It is reformism without reforms, a 'social democracy' which celebrates being bourgeois more than social and authoritarian rather than democratic.

In addition, all this was before the government embarked on a political showdown with the Fire Brigades Union, replete with threats to ban strikes, with ministerial characterisations of the firefighters as 'criminal' and with vetoes of agreements between the union and the employers. That dispute had the consequence of uniting, at long last, almost the whole trade union movement against the government. It also brought back to the forefront of debate an issue which has long been a bugbear of the establishment – trade unions' involvement in politics and, specifically, their relationship to the Labour Party. This hostility is fuelled by deep-seated class contempt. While bourgeois democracy has ultimately come to accept that working-class individuals have the right to participate in the political process, the idea of the working class doing so collectively, through the medium of their own organisations, remains anathema.

For example, Simon Jenkins wrote in *The Times* that he had discovered that the Fire Brigades Union website described the union's 'ultimate aim of bringing about the socialist system' and then added 'what this has to do with fires is a mystery'. Jenkins' quip, which he doubtless considered a highly clever contribution to the demonising of the firefighters, merely shows that he has missed the point of trade unions almost completely. To follow his example, the FBU is not an organisation for putting out fires. That is the role of the Fire Service, in which its members work. The FBU is a collective of working men and women, in this case defined by a particular employment, for advancing their interests at work and in society at large. Mr Jenkins' ignorance of this distinction could be underlined by endless, more strident, examples.[18]

Since the earliest days of mass trade unionism, the establishment has been concerned to confine the unions to purely industrial and self-help functions, since those on their own cannot challenge the fundamental pillars of the capitalist system. Yet even limited legislative improvements to working life cannot be achieved through industrially-based activity alone, a reality which prompted trade unions to take the lead in the creation of the Labour Party. The fact that Labour, which has been either in government or official opposition for the last eighty years or so, has rested on the affiliation of trade unions and remains largely funded by them, has generally been viewed by Conservatism as little less than a violation of constitutional order. A variety of measures – from the post-General Strike legislation requiring individual members to 'opt in' to the payment of the political fund which their union may have collectively established, up to the 1980's law mandating regular ballots on the maintenance of such funds – have been devised to try and break that connection.

The parallel ideological attack on the link has been just as impor-tant. Even when trade unions have been at their most moderate, big business has never been reconciled to their affiliation to the Labour Party and attacks on the 'block vote' and 'Labour's paymasters' have been a stock-in-trade of Conservative punditry down the years.

Yet in the last ten years the Labour–union connection has become a source of controversy within the movement as great as it was previously between Labour and its political opponents. From the beginning of 'the project', as the Blair–Brown coup within the Labour Party was known, either ending the union link or attenuating it to the point where only a symbolic remnant remains has been a central goal. This alone could ensure that Labour seemed 'safe' to middle England focus groups, which, under the new regime, was the measure of all things.

Decoupling was pursued with zeal in New Labour's early years. Stephen Byers was dispatched to Blackpool during a TUC congress to brief journalists that getting shot of the unions completely was one of the new Party leadership's objectives. This formed a part of Blair's bid to woo the Thatcherite press and the City in advance of his first election victory.

The place given on the New Labour agenda to cutting the unions out from the Party they created has since fluctuated. It has, however, never gone away and has recently re-emerged with a vengeance. This time, however, it is those in the unions themselves and on the left who are questioning the continuing utility of funding Labour.

The major public service unions were deeply unhappy at the way Blair announced his determination to introduce private capital into public services in the course of the 2001 election campaign – both at the substance of the policy and the complete lack of any preceding consultation. The inability of the government to straighten out this issue led in time to Blair being defeated at the Labour Conference in 2002 over a demand for a review on the role of Private Finance Initiatives in public services – only his second such conference defeat as leader. The union anger over this and other issues has since become palpable, reinforced by ministers' vituperative attacks on the Fire Brigades Union in the course of their pay and conditions dispute.

John Edmonds of the GMB told the *Daily Mirror* in January 2002: 'My union has supported Labour candidates in every election since it was founded more than 100 years ago. But no longer can the Party take the support of our members for granted', particularly over privatisation.[19] Bill Morris, T&G General Secretary, wrote in his union journal in December 2002 that the 'dividing line between the parties seemed to be blurred if not erased altogether', and added in April 2003 that many of his members were questioning whether it was actually better to have a Labour government.

Even John Monks, who could not have tried harder to reconcile union hopes with Blair's intent to ignore them, was moved to comment in March 2002: 'We know it is not just a trade union government. It must get on with the best of British business. We are up for deals, for social partnership with employers, and for change in public services. But let's not have to repeat a variation on the famous Kinnock charge … that a Labour government, a Labour government, let us down applying the values of social democracy.'[20]

The government's handling of the fire service dispute drove even Monks to exasperation. For the first time in ten years, the TUC organised a national demonstration on an industrial issue – in support of the FBU and against the government. But even here there was a weakness – as soon as the government determined to make the dispute 'political' which, given it was a consequence of political decisions, it inevitably was, the TUC started looking for a way out. Convinced of the constitutional impropriety of challenging politicians in their own sphere, the right-wing at Congress House began looking for peace at any price.

While this may not have greatly helped the Fire Brigades Union, nor did it help to reconcile the unions to a continuation of their subordinate and supplicatory role within the Party. The future of the link was back at the centre of debate.

Labour's own General Secretary, David Triesman, himself a former union leader, warned that the unions and Labour might be 'sleepwalking' into a separation because of their differences. He described this prospect as a 'catastrophe', although he was less than ingenuous in adding that 'nobody in the leadership of the party or government has raised questions about the historic link'. In fact, they have done so regularly since the inception of the New Labour project.[21]

If the Blair group is quieter on the issue now, it is in large part because they fear for the future funding of the Party. With the introduction of state funding politically problematic, individual Party membership falling rapidly and the Prime Minister damaged by repeated scandals over donations from rich admirers, there is no short-term alternative to financial support from the unions. But the Prime Minister's objective of removing the last connections of class from his 'one nation' Party surely remains.

There are still, however, some right-wingers who might see an advantage in retaining the Labour–union link in order to make it easier to impose unpopular policies on the workforce. Former Labour special adviser David Clark argued that 'it is only through an acceptance of a broader political responsibility that unions can be expected to exercise the self-restraint required to sacrifice short-term sectional interests in the pursuit of longer-term national objectives'. Blair's approach, Clark warned, 'will be to encourage precisely the sort of industrial militancy Labour needs least'. Put like that, the unions are being invited to a re-run of the Wilson–Callaghan experience when the assumption of political responsibility without political power led to the setbacks for both unions and Party described above.[22]

So what is the future? There is little support among the new leaders of the trade unions for ending the link with Labour, however, it would be foolish to pretend that sympathy for the notion is not growing. The virulent attacks by the government on the firefighters and the widespread opposition to the war against Iraq, when added to specific industrial sources of discontent – over transport policy in the RMT rail union, for example – are making disaffiliation an unavoidable issue at many union conferences.

It is clearly untenable to maintain affiliation on the terms set down by, for example, Peter Mandelson. The former minister and continuing Blair confidante wrote in *Progress*, the Labour right-wing's house journal, that 'the future strength of the Labour–union link depends on the unions acting on a shared understanding that they should not abuse their privileged place within Labour's constitution to coerce the government or manipulate its policies'. To underline the point, he stressed that this meant accepting the government line on public sector wages, labour market regulation (or lack of it) and public service 'reform' – privatisation. In other words, they had to sign up to the whole Blair agenda on core union issues without qualification.[23]

If the union leaderships were to acquiesce in that approach, their members would decide, sooner rather than later, to sever the link with Labour. Perhaps that is what Mandelson himself, a long-standing advocate of eventually breaking the link, would like.

Challenging New Labour, and seeking to return the Party to something like a 'real Labour' perspective is the only way to keep the union link alive. Whether such a shift in Labour's policy can still be attained is at the heart of the debate within the rising left in the unions.

A split would hardly serve the trade union interest. They would lose whatever leverage they have, and any prospect of extending it in future, in return for – what? If the unions are collectively not strong enough to impose their will in the Labour Party, then they are scarcely likely to be strong enough to pursue any other political course of action with any likelihood of success. Indeed, it is hard to imagine that the major affiliated unions would even agree on what 'Plan B' might look like. The most probable consequence of unions breaking with Labour would be a drift to a US-style political approach on behalf of organised labour, with unions following a policy agenda on an issue-by-issue basis. The Liberal Democrats might be one beneficiary of that approach – the TUC under Monks even held discussions with the Tories on the pensions crisis.

The Scottish Socialist Party, which emerged from mass campaigning against the Poll Tax north of the border, has developed as a credible electoral alternative to Labour in circumstances where proportional representation makes securing seats in the Scottish parliament a realistic objective. It has, however, not secured any organised and official trade union backing.

Left-wing electoral alternatives to Labour in England and Wales have all foundered. The Socialist Labour Party, despite Arthur Scargill's personal prestige, has been bedevilled by factionalism and has lost whatever union support it ever had, without making an electoral impact outside a small number of constituencies. The Socialist Alliance, which unites the Socialist Workers Party with a number of very small Trotskyist groups, has not managed to extend its active core much beyond the far-left and, again, its electoral results have been modest. No major union, at national level at least, is going to be attracted by these or similar ventures. To the extent that such endeavours win the support of individual socialists, they risk undermining the great achievement of the Labour Party's formation – bringing the mass working-class organisations and the socialist groups into a common electoral front. Socialists without trade unionists tend to be sterile and sectarian, while a trade union party without socialists would lack any coherence in addressing the broader problems of society. A union–Labour divorce would look very like an historic setback for working-class politics.

Similar problems attend suggestions that the union political funds should be either broken up and dispersed among a variety of political parties, or devolved to local control. Both ideas risk dissolving the unions as collective organisations in the political field. They raise the possibility – not a fanciful one – of the same union supporting competing candidates in a given election, and certainly of different unions doing so. The unified political voice of the working class would thus be reduced to a cacophony. These ideas are advocated under the rubric of 'democratising' the use of the political funds. But fragmentation is not the same as democratisation – the decision to use the funds nationally to affiliate to Labour is as democratic as any other decisions taken by unions in conformity with their own rules.

But none of these considerations make the *status quo* sustainable. Taking the Labour Party back from the Blair–Brown right-wing group is not a job for another day – and there is more than the beginnings of a trade union stirring. A range of government policies, from support for the US war against Iraq to the creeping privatisation of the public services, are opposed in the movement (and society as a whole) by a far wider group than the traditional left or the 'usual suspects'.

The union challenge to privatisation of the public services was powerful and not unexpected, since it merges a policy issue with direct industrial concerns. More remarkable, and perhaps just as worrying for New Labour, was the preponderant opposition to Blair's war policy. The 2002 TUC saw a parade of union leaders, including most of the newly-elected left-wingers, challenge the government on its plans to attack Iraq in alliance with George Bush, and dismiss a Congress House fudge designed, as ever, to get Downing Street off the hook. While the TUC may try to split the emerging left and make the movement safe for the ministers, this has little chance of success unless it coincides with real changes in government policy. The refusal of the government to consider any further changes in UK employment legislation, announced in March 2003, and its failure to impose an obligation of consultation on employers in line with EU directives, decided in April, (both to applause from the CBI) will have further strengthened the case for a more confrontational approach towards the Blairites.

Even the Communist Party, and its associated newspaper the *Morning Star*, has been gaining ground in this milieu. The *New Statesman*, reviewing the 2002 TUC, wrote that 'the communists are providing an organisational focus for the rising wave of angry young leaders' and that they were all keen to be associated with the *Star* and its policies of opposition to privatisation and war. The Communist Party argues for maintaining the unity of the labour movement while fighting to defeat New Labour within its structures.

Some trade unionists have hoped that a Gordon Brown succession to the Party leadership will make life easier for the unions. This is an illusion of heroic proportions which requires, *inter alia*, ignoring the Chancellor's oft-declared admiration for US-style capitalism in the raw, something he has carried into British politics with his demand that schoolchildren be taught to admire business leaders as role models.

'I want every young person to hear about business enterprise in school, every teacher to be able to communicate the virtues of business', he said. The uproar which would have ensued had the Chancellor substituted 'socialism' or 'trade unionism' for business in that formulation may easily be imagined![24]

At a more practical level, he has introduced student loans instead of grants (something which is linked to an apparent increase in student prostitution), the insulting 75p increase paid to state pensioners, the disastrous part-privatisation of the London Underground, the decision to stick to Tory spending plans for the first two years of the Labour government, which stored up so much trouble for later on, the drive to extend the Private Finance Initiative throughout public services – and so on. Whatever this is, it is not a 'real Labour' record. The political columnist for *The Times*, Peter Riddell, has aptly described Brown as 'new Labour policy in old Labour language' and adds that the Chancellor, like the Prime Minister, has embraced capitalism.[25] Indeed, when the chips are down, as in the FBU dispute or over war against Iraq, the once-senior partner in what was originally known as the Brown–Blair project is as one with the present premier.

So defeating New Labour means more than a personnel change at the very top. It means bringing centre-ground Labour figures like Robin Cook, Frank Dobson, Glenda Jackson and Peter Kilfoyle into a 'reclaim Labour' alliance with the unions and the left on a policy which, initially, would need to focus only on a very few key questions – peace, defence of public services and elementary measures of an egalitarian nature.

Ironically, the broad left attitude towards the union relationship with Labour was best expressed by the FBU's Andy Gilchrist at the very moment when ministers were abusing him most heatedly. He had gone to a Socialist Campaign Group conference in Manchester in the midst of the dispute and called, amongst other things, for socialists not to abandon Labour but instead seek to replace 'New Labour' with 'real Labour'. For this piece of sound sense he was attacked by Pensions Minister Ian McCartney – always available to the government when New Labour nonsense needs an old Labour gloss and now promoted to Party Chairman as a reward for his efforts – for having 'lost the plot.' Gilchrist elaborated his point in the *Guardian*:

> My call on Saturday was simply to work within the constitution of Labour to reclaim the party for socialist values and pro-working class policies... if we fail in these objectives, the Labour Party will be lost to its new Labour colonisers and the organic unity between party and unions will be destroyed ... If that were to happen it would be a bleak day for working people and the Labour Party. The party's unique strength is its links in the organised working class. Through its federal structures the party can, if it chooses, reflect the experiences and aspirations of millions of working people. It is Labour's direct link to the factory floor, to the housing estate, to the experiences of millions working in the public sector ... if Labour were to abandon it, the party would become just another rudderless organisation totally controlled by the professional political class.[26]

Gilchrist puts the point very clearly. Yet not everyone on the left, or even amongst the new union leaders is convinced. Nor do unions live in a different world to individual Labour members. At the time of writing, Party membership is falling fast, and as many as 70,000 members (around one quarter of the total) were reported to be ready to resign if the government joined in an attack on Iraq. As *Tribune* editor Mark Seddon – a Labour national executive member – has written, there is a deepening 'schism between real Labour and the new Labour elite which now dominates the party'.[27]

The next few years – maybe the next one or two – are likely to be decisive. Either the unions can, in alliance with constituency activists, reassert Labour as the political vehicle for working-class interests, or the disintegration will prove irreversible. Since it cannot be emphasised too often that unions can only achieve a fraction of their broad objectives through industrial means alone, there is no more decisive challenge facing the trade union movement today than getting the politics right.

6

Organising, Equality and Internationalism

Even if the trade union movement were to get its politics right, there are other issues which urgently need to be addressed before it can really play the part demanded of it.

Three issues, in particular, demand attention: the need to organise millions of workers presently outside trade unions, which must include the development of an alternative to the discredited 'social partnership' model; the continuing imperative to ensure equality within the movement for women and black people; and the requirement for a new approach to internationalism in an evolving world economy. A more general vision of the role of the labour movement in society and the development by the movement of social, economic and political alternatives to the world as it is, can only rest on progress on these questions.

Organising the New

Think of the typical trade unionist today. You almost certainly have the wrong picture in mind.

He is a white-collar worker, probably a professional in his mid-forties. Yet think of the typical employee today and – well, he is a she for a start. And more likely to be blue-collar, low-waged and, particularly in the private sector, not a member of a union.

The ravages of the last twenty years have changed not just the number of trade unionists – now around 7.3 million, including those few in non-TUC affiliates, down from over thirteen million at its 1979 peak – but their nature as well.

Every time a car plant closes, every time a textile firm ships east in search of cheaper labour, every time a badly-managed communications company lays off another thousand or so workers, it is likely that a traditional centre of trade unionism has been destroyed or at least diminished.

And every time an out-of-town supermarket opens, a financial services company extends its business, a high-tech start-up starts up, or Starbucks launches another twenty-five outlets, the trade union movement is presented with an organising challenge it has not, traditionally, been very good at meeting.

Why, for example, are only 16 per cent of employees of Pakistani or Bangladeshi origin members of trade unions? These workers are largely concentrated in the worst-paying jobs and often, in sweatshop industries, also endure the most Dickensian workplace conditions. Start the futile search for a national union leader with the same background, and you might get part of the answer. But only a part, because non-unionism is far from being confined to workers from South Asia. According to the Labour Force Survey, barely 5 per cent of workers in hotels and restaurants are union members; only 11 per cent in wholesale and retail; just one in five in construction – and under half even in health and social work.[28]

Some still argue that, in Britain's flexible go-getting new economy, employees don't really need trade unions like they used to. Both anecdotes and statistics tell a different story.

One of the interviews with a union leader for this book was conducted in an office where the union rents space in London's West End. The receptionist – not a union employee, but working for a contract firm – had just started a twelve-hour shift for the fourth day running. That's twelve hours without a break. She was allowed as far as the front door for a breath of fresh air, but that was it. Minimum wage. Her employer, she told me, 'didn't allow unions'.

More than one in five workers in Britain now work *unpaid* overtime each week – an average of seven hours a week, worth more than £5,000 a year of free labour to their boss.[29] Over 750,000 women workers are working hours in excess of the European Union's 48-a-week limit, set down in the Working Time Directive – in the public sector as well as the private. Around five million people still earn less than £250 a week. Three million workers were not paid for taking Christmas Day 2002 off from work!

Do these workers want trade unions and can the unions do anything for them? The concern over pension provision (and the receptionist mentioned above is one of millions who have never been in sight of a pension scheme to begin with) is one example of how both questions can be answered positively. One major employer after another has been cutting pension provisions for its workforce, while ensuring, of course, that the boardroom remains well looked after. Trade unions have never stopped reminding employees that pensions are, in fact, deferred wages, set aside by workers themselves for their retirement, not fringe benefits to be conceded or withdrawn by employers at their pleasure. As of December 2002, 55 per cent of final salary schemes had been closed to new entrants over the preceding five years, including at blue-chip companies like British Airways and Sainsbury's.

The GMB's Cath Unsworth points out that many companies were happy to take a break from contributing to pension schemes in the prosperous years of the 1990s. Such firms are 'all reneging on their promise. Instead of biting the bullet and putting up their contribution, they're saying "silly me, didn't realise that's the flip side".'

All the major unions have identified pensions as a critical issue; amicus has said that 'the main battleground for the future in terms of industrial relations is not going to be pay any more but pensions', although pensions are actually a part of wages themselves. ASLEF has warned train companies that it will strike if pension schemes are tampered with. The ISTC took successful action at Caparo, a Scunthorpe engineering firm owned by Labour peer Lord Paul, in order to keep their pension scheme. 'We were the first and we won't be the last', a union spokesman said.

Unions at the British subsidiary of US agricultural machinery firm Agco took the legal route, and won a challenge to a company decision to cut pension benefits for some workers who had been made redundant. If unions are consistently seen as defending pension provision then that will not only be of obvious benefit to existing members, but will also establish the desirability of union membership among groups of workers perhaps not immediately concerned about their pay or working conditions.

There are plenty of other examples of imaginative trade union engagement with the problems of organising in a changing workforce. Unison, for example, has worked with The East London Communities Organisation on a living wage campaign in some of the most deprived boroughs in Britain. The aim has been to ensure that public bodies in the NHS and elsewhere make contractors pay their workers a 'London Living Wage' of £6.30 an hour. According to TELCO organiser Catherine Howarth 'the project is also aimed at increasing recruitment into the union, developing leaders and activists within the workplace and in the community, and raising awareness of low pay'. Victories have been achieved – the cleaning service at one school in Leytonstone has been taken back in-house from a poor-paying contractor, and cleaners' pay raised to £6.50 an hour from £4.18, thanks to TELCO. The campaign is a template for bringing a wide range of religious and community groups together with union branches around joint demands.

The GMB has launched a campaign to encourage both employers and unions themselves to regard domestic violence as a workplace issue. Called the Daphne Project, it has involved distributing information with pay slips on an issue which union organisers of a previous generation would have run a mile from raising. The GMB's Karen Constantine says that the initiative has helped recruitment because 'appealing to women on women's issues not only makes us attractive and interesting to women, but also … makes us more visible. We know that particularly outside the public sector women workers under the age of 35–40 have a very limited knowledge of trade unions either in role or function. The GMB has also found that this project has encouraged women members into new roles in the union.'

The T&G has successfully targeted a recruitment campaign within the textile industry, mainly organising women workers, a high proportion of them Asian. 'These workers had a distrust of unions and, indeed, some had felt they had been let down by unions in the past and therefore believed that, although they were being treated badly at work, unions were not the vehicle for change', says Sharon Graham, the T&G's youth and recruitment officer and a graduate of the TUC's

Organising Academy. 'Before the push for recognition could begin, it was necessary to break down these stereotypes, bring forward workplace contacts that reflected the diversity of the workforce and give confidence to these workers. It had to be shown that the union was there for the long haul. We also involved Asian stewards from similar workplaces ... and providing regular communication via response leaflets in both English and Urdu.' The result was an 89 per cent vote for union recognition in the particular workplace.[30]

However, for all these examples and more, the trade union movement is doing no better than standing still. Every recession makes tens of thousands of union members redundant in manufacturing, construction and other long-organised industries. Every boom sees new jobs created in smaller workplaces and newer industries. It takes a lot of organisers a lot of time to recruit enough members to cover the losses from just one big factory closure. The unions can run very fast indeed without moving any further forward.

Perhaps lessons need to be learned from the trade unions in the USA and elsewhere. The major affiliates of the AFL-CIO devote a much bigger share of their annual budgets to recruitment and organising – typically more than a quarter, sometimes much more. In Britain, by contrast, most of the considerable resources at the disposal of the big unions are spent on administration and the servicing of the existing membership. In most cases, less than 5 per cent is set aside for recruitment activities, although more than half of trade unions do now employ specialist organisers.

The TUC has given a lead on this issue. It established the Organising Academy to train union organisers in 1997, a project which has sent around 150 skilled recruiters (most of them young) out into the movement. This has got results: the Iron and Steel Trades

Confederation used Academy trainees to spearhead organising drives taking the union out of its declining strongholds in the steel industry, and one Academy graduate working for the GPMU, Jamie Major, has won over 900 members for the union in a branch in southern England – half the working membership of the branch.[31]

The TUC has maintained this focus on the need to organise. John Monks addressed a packed conference at Congress House on the theme *Organising: the future of work – the future of unions* in November 2002. The unions, he said 'have the best opportunity in a generation to grow again', but he identified the problems sharply, too: insufficient commitment of resources, 'young people remaining on the fringes of the movement' and the fact that many union officers 'get more satisfaction from negotiating, servicing and the representing side of the job than they do from the hard graft of recruiting'. The unions had a desperate need to 'go beyond our core audiences', he said, adding that 'the scale of the challenge is daunting'.[32]

However, the tension between representing the existing, and diminishing, membership and putting resources into recruiting in new areas is only one of the choices confronting unions. The other is whether they are trying to grow as independent, democratic, working-class organisations, or through marketing themselves to employers. Both strategies co-exist, increasingly uneasily, within the trade union movement. During the Tory years, when wringing union recognition out of recalcitrant employers was exceptionally difficult, unions sometimes concentrated on promoting themselves as a solution to Human Resource Management problems for companies, never mind what the workers themselves may have thought. 'Beauty contests' between different unions to persuade an employer to grant them sole recognition rights became a new feature of trade union life. The competition hinged, obviously, on which union the employer could induce or coerce into signing the most pliable agreement. The case of the Nissan car plant in Sunderland, where the then AEU secured a single-union deal with the employer, but for years could not persuade as many as one worker in ten actually to join the union, is one example of the fruits of that approach.

The very title chosen by the TUC for its organising work – the New Unionism Project – reflects this ambiguity. Is that 'new unionism' as in the original 'new unionism' of the 1880s, which saw trade unionism extended to unskilled workers in a series of celebrated industrial confrontations, or 'new unionism' as in 'New Labour'?

It depends who you speak to. John Monks launched the TUC's Partnership Institute – a body set up to help unions and employers make friendly with each other – in 2000 with the assurance that 'unions can be a boost to business. Partnership makes managers take their workforce with them. This is no burden on business but the secret to success. I have always said unions must be part of the solution, not part of the problem.' TUC official Sarah Veale responded to the news that a law firm had organised seminars for businesses on importing US union-busting techniques into Britain with the following apology: 'It is worrying that there are a number of well-known companies that are still sufficiently anxious about trade unions to be part of this. If they bothered to talk directly to trade unions they would realise how attitudes have changed.' And the head of the TUC's economics department, David Coates, assured *Progress* readers that the unions have not 'abandoned their strategic commitment to social partnership in favour of a crude industrial militancy' and that it would be wrong to conclude from the resurgence in strikes in 2002 'that an aggressive and confrontational strategy is the right one'.[33]

A different mood increasingly prevails away from Congress House. The views of Derek Simpson have already been noted. In addition, the T&G's Tony Woodley won election as his union's General Secretary with a clear message: 'if we fight, we may not always win, if we don't fight, we will surely lose' and 'the T&G is not about being a business union, but about doing the business for the members'.[34] That is the attitude winning trade unionists' votes today. It is not a programme for endless industrial action, but an outlook which acknowledges that there is an inevitable conflict of interest between employer and employee and that, if unions are ambivalent as to where they stand in that conflict, they will eventually write themselves out of a role.

It is now easier for unions to win recognition, thanks to the legislative changes introduced by Labour since 1997. While the procedures laid down are cumbersome and only barely democratic (companies can secure injunctions to block the process if they think the rules have been broken, but unions cannot, for example), they do make it harder for employers to evade collective representation by the workforce. However, relying on this new law alone will not necessarily produce the breakthrough unions require. *Guardian* columnist Polly Toynbee did worry that 'joining a union in the multiplying workplaces with zero trade union tradition is almost impossible … trade unionism may now be in a terminal decline, caught in a vicious spiral where fewer members mean less manpower [*sic*] for recruiting new ones. Yet a casualised, contracted out, more insecure workforce needs union protection now more than ever.'[35] It is exactly those changes in the workforce, combined with the entrenched attitudes of many unions, based on methods which achieved results in previous decades in different labour markets, which make the task of organisation so hard.

Michael Crosby of the Australian trade unions has put the issue well:

> Organising is about much more than putting resources into growth and getting a few new members. It is in fact a profound change in the way that every part of the union does its business. It involves the development, education and mobilisation of large numbers of members in doing the work of the union ... an organisation that gives power to members to stand up for them-selves. Recognition ballots too can be seductive in encouraging organisers to see them as an end in themselves ... winning the ballot certainly doesn't mean that workers are powerful. Once the ballot is over, unless organising continues, they will go straight back to feeling powerless in the face of employer intimidation.[36]

Can unions make that 'profound change' and build lasting organi-sation in the new workplaces? Possibly their future as a social, rather than a sectional, movement depends on the answer to that question. Tomorrow's unions need to be as deeply-rooted in the diverse – in terms of occupation, race, gender, terms-of-employment – workforce of the twenty-first century as they once were in the more monolithic workforce of the past, or they risk a continued marginalisation.

Looking Like the Workforce

For a moment, the present looked like the future should. The Transport and General Workers Union entered the new millennium with a black man as its General Secretary, and a woman as his deputy – both directly elected by the membership of a union perhaps more embedded in the history of the twentieth-century labour movement in Britain than any other.

But was the eminence of Bill Morris and Margaret Prosser more than a fluke? All the candidates to replace each of them on their retirement were white men. Look further down the ranks of T&G officialdom and the picture is not encouraging. The union's nineteen national officials below the top two jobs included in December 2002 just two women (one of them black), serving as national organiser and national secretary for the equalities sector, and no black men. And the T&G is one of the better unions – under Morris, it has grasped the equality nettle more firmly than most, and used reserved seats to considerably boost the number of women serving on the union's General Executive Council.

Other unions have taken similar steps, but the top of the movement is still a white man's club. Post-Morris and Prosser, an objective listing of the thirty most important union officials in the country would reveal nobody black and just two women, the deputy general secretaries of the TUC and the GMB, Frances O'Grady and Debbie Coulter respectively.

The greatest vehemence I encountered in the interviews for this book was expressed by the two women I interviewed – Heather Wakefield of Unison and Rozanne Foyer of the Scottish TUC – in relation to the treatment of their gender in the movement. It is in large part the anger that comes from having to repeat the same simple truth over and over again, find no serious argument against it, and then still find, *year after year*, that little changes. While trade unions now by-and-large have state-of-the art policies in relation to women's equality at work and in society, they remain, not merely no better than, but in some cases worse than many of the employers they deal with in terms of their own practices. Too many unions have proved unwilling to translate those policies into action when it would touch upon the power relationships in their own union or, perhaps, in the lives of their own officials. As a consequence, as Fabian Society pamphleteer Jane Willis puts it, 'as though in a time capsule for the last 30 years, the public see trade unions fronted by ageing white men with a strong smell of engineering oil about them. Union hierarchies ill-reflect the feminised, racially diverse, service-sector population working in Britain today.'[37]

Advance on equality questions has proved more intractable than any other, perhaps because the entrenched male-led bureaucratic hierarchies of most union organisations still manage, perhaps unwittingly, to freeze a good non-sexist policy dead at a hundred paces. The TUC set a good example in January 2003 when it filled the second and third spots in its own hierarchy with women. But no affiliate, with factions and votes in place of the TUC's best-practice procedures, has achieved as much.

What more can be done when the policies and procedures are all in place, on paper at least? Imaginative campaigning on issues like breast cancer screening or domestic violence, to take the example mentioned above, are part of the answer, at least as far as recruitment is concerned. The TUC's active engagement in community-based anti-racist campaigning in the 1990s is another positive example, although this has not overcome the great lack of black faces in union leaderships, nor on its own eroded the distrust of unions accumulated among black people through decades in which racist employment practices at grass-roots level were sometimes connived at.

There is no black union leader interviewed for this book. That is because, with the retirement of Bill Morris from the top job at the

T&G in October 2003, there won't be one (excepting Beverley Barnard, the US-born woman running the Royal College of Nursing, a non-TUC affiliate). There is no sense in which this can be anything but an indictment of the trade union movement, not one, but two generations after large-scale Asian and Afro-Caribbean immigration (almost entirely working-class) became a fact of British life. The extent to which this devalues the progressive position taken by trade unions on race equality issues, and undermines the demands it makes on society and business on behalf of black workers, should not be underestimated.

The interviews here with Heather Wakefield and Rozanne Foyer are suggestive of answers as far as the involvement of women are concerned. Heather outlines how women have become more active in Unison in a variety of ways as a result of the industrial action taken throughout local authorities in summer 2002. Struggle can still help propel changes in ways that policy alone cannot – the little tale of the strike at Dolphin Square is included here because it illustrates this point in relation to a section of the workforce which unions desperately need to organise. A culture within unions which ceased to tolerate behaviour by its own officials which it would refuse to accept in employers would address the problem raised by Rozanne of women being driven out of official union positions by such conduct. Not all women are, of course, so excluded, but such episodes are far more than occasional and in some cases only minimised by women officials adapting, as Rozanne suggests, to the prevailing pattern of male (mis)conduct.

As with the other challenges, this one cannot be ducked for much longer. Women now account for more than half the workforce and are concentrated in sections, like retail and catering, with low levels of union density. The millions of unorganised low-paid workers include a very high proportion of Britain's black population. If the union movement obstinately refuses to make room for a more visibly diverse leadership, it risks looking increasingly anachronistic. This is not only bad for women and black workers themselves, but it will cripple the effectiveness of the movement as a whole. The time cannot be far off when only a far-reaching programme of positive discrimination, for full-time as well as lay positions, is embraced as part of the solution.

A World to Win

May Day celebrations in London were pretty flat for many years. Seldom a public holiday because the Callaghan government had opted to give the nation's workers the nearest Monday off as a Bank Holiday, rather than international workers' day itself, the annual demonstration organised by the trade union movement in the city where Karl Marx had convened the First International had long been small and uninspiring. Only the capital's Turkish and Kurdish communities turned out in any force. Internationalism appeared not to loom large for the huge majority of British workers, the young in particular.

The year 2002 was different. The London labour movement, despite ill-disguised anxiety from some in the TUC hierarchy, took what felt like a risk and agreed to co-organise the event with Globalise Resistance, the political end of the worldwide anti-globalisation movement in Britain. The day was transformed – thousands of young people joined the official May Day march for the first time in many years and heard a varied selection of speakers address a large rally in Trafalgar Square. The trade union movement felt lively and interesting.

The anti-globalisation movement which began to arise in the late 1990s had appeared to live on a different planet to the labour movement – to the detriment of both. The anti-capitalist demonstrators who took their protests – over world poverty, the environment, peace, trade and other issues – to one summit of the rich and powerful after another around the world, have a demonstrably global outlook, where unions appear insular. They appeal to younger people, while unions, by and large, do not. Yet unions retain the potential to shake governments and make ruling classes shudder (as the relatively small example of the firefighters' dispute illustrated), while often the protests at G7 gatherings tended to underline the truth of Eric Hobsbawm's aphorism, struck in relation to *les événements* of 1968, that 'shocking the bourgeois is, alas, easier than overthrowing him'.[38]

Unions should be the natural vehicle for an effective anti-capitalism, although they would first need to stop cuddling up to capitalists. But the movement against capitalist globalisation has, in Britain certainly and to a large extent elsewhere, developed in isolation from them. Yet the issues it raises are of vital importance for the 'traditional' labour movement. While the last twenty years have increasingly seen capital 'go global', the trade unions have stayed local, and it shows. Cross-border mergers between companies, the wholesale relocation of production (and in some cases services) to low-cost countries and the erosion of barriers to the movement of goods and money have all been signal aspects of the new economic environment, which at every stage of their development have swept away the jobs of hundreds of thousands of union-organised workers in Britain. The trade unions have not been slow to recognise this, but translating awareness into action has thus far proved an all-but intractable problem. Certainly, the anti-corporate message of rallies like those in cities from Seattle to Genoa sits uneasily with the pallid dogmas of 'social partnership'.

The British labour movement has a fine tradition of international solidarity, still alive today – exemplified in practical and political solidarity with trade unionists in Colombia, where to represent workers is to invite a death sentence. But this solidarity has seldom intruded into the practical conduct of industrial business – nor has it in the trade unions of other countries either. Finding the ways to do so will prove vital to re-establishing the power of labour in today's world economy. The 'anti-capitalist' movement's contribution here lies in asserting the political primacy of global questions over national ones for any movement seeking social change.

It is six years since progressive US journalist William Greider published his ground-breaking survey of the emerging world economy under the title *One World – Ready or Not*. As far as unions in Britain – and elsewhere – were concerned, it was definitely a case of 'not'. Yet having examined the interstices of global capitalism, the movement of jobs and production around the world, and the new social relations and conflicts this engendered, Greider's conclusion – 'if organised labour does not wither and disappear, as some expect, it will have to reinvent itself' – is a compelling one. He adds: 'If the established industrial unions expect to speak for exploited others at the far end of the global economy, they will first have to rediscover their own original social conscience and re-educate their own members and societies about what is both right and necessary in this new world.'[39]

There are certainly considerable problems with the idea of cross-border trade union mergers, something explicitly floated here by Derek Simpson. Labour operates under different legal jurisdictions, governing both the conduct of industrial relations and the status of unions themselves. Building a democratic international working-class organisation would have to overcome those, as well as the problem of language. It is also the case that political power and state resources still remain overwhelmingly located at the level of the nation-state. Pressurising or transforming that power, and accessing those resources, are inevitably central social objectives of the labour movement.

Yet it remains a glaring and damaging incongruity that while businesses are merging across countries and even continents, unions often struggle to consolidate at national level, never mind establishing practical and functioning counter-weights to the power of money internationally. The inadequacy of existing international trade union organisations is patent, even where there are good intentions.

For example, the International Metalworkers Federation, one of the most active union 'internationals', organised a study conference once every three years or so for journalists employed by its national affiliates. As a then-employee of the Transport and General Workers Union, I was lucky enough to attend one in the USA and Mexico in 1993. The trip was designed to highlight the issues raised by the crumbling of trade barriers and the movement of manufacturing jobs to low-wage locations. A better site could not have been selected than the US–Mexican border. Crossing from San Diego on the Californian side to Tijuana on the Mexican side took about an hour – and took you back 150 years or more in terms of social development. But not industrial development. Amid the shanty town squalor on the Mexican side of the border were gleaming new assembly plants owned by brand-name Trans-National Corporations, producing for export back to the USA.

All this had been made possible by the North American Free Trade Area, joining the economies of Canada and Mexico to that of the

USA, which had just been signed. There was just one striking drawback to the whole event, which dramatised the issues facing trade unionists in rapidly-integrating regional and global economies. It is that while national affiliates throughout Western Europe and North America were represented at the conference, there was not a single union journalist from Latin America, Asia, Africa or Eastern Europe. They could not afford to be there, and no one had thought to subsidise their attendance – yet there could be no solution to the issues raised by the trip without their engagement.

In general, international union organisations play a very limited role. Shaped by the anti-Soviet imperatives of the Cold War, international federations remain, with the International Transport Workers Federation as an honourable exception, remote from practical struggles, while European-wide federations are most often lobbying adjuncts of the EU's considerable bureaucracy. Often non-governmental organisations play a far more vigorous campaigning role on issues like world trade and poverty. Cross-border shop stewards contacts have developed in a few companies, but they are far from being a widespread or dynamic form of organisation at present.

The imperatives of working-class internationalism now stretch beyond the traditions of solidarity with the oppressed or those in difficult circumstances much closer to the heart of day-to-day union business. Communities of production now no longer huddle around a pithead or at a shipyard's gates, but stretch across countries and continents.

Organising therefore needs to become international. Leading industrial relations academic John Kelly has highlighted the example of US clothing and textile unions helping the organisation of workers used as cheap labour in Central and South America – areas to which many US textile firms have relocated production. Kelly also set out, in a pamphlet published by the TUC, important ideas for developing the range of actions unions can deploy in this new environment: 'The traditional power resource of organised workers – the withdrawal of labour – needs to be supplemented with additional weapons if workers' terms and conditions are to be defended and improved ... they fall under four headings: international solidarity action involving workers from other countries; coalitions with campaigning groups and social movements; accessing political power at local, national and international levels; and corporate campaigns designed to divide employers and shareholders.'[40]

In respect of some of these ideas, groups associated with the large and amorphous 'anti-capitalist' movement worldwide have shown a lead – pressurising Nike, for example, to set minimum labour standards for those employed on poverty wages in the factories of its sub-contractors. This imagination needs, however, to be harnessed to the power of organised labour if it is to reap a harvest of a lasting change in the balance of power in the international economy.

PART TWO

Awkward Voices

1

Changing the Guard on Planet Zog

Many Conservatives have always treated militant trade unionism as akin to an alien invasion. New Labour Employment Minister Alan Johnson had alarming news for them in April 2003. 'The TUC left planet Zog 20-odd years ago, but a few union leaders go back for the occasional day trip', he told a newspaper reporter in the most outspoken ministerial attack on the new left.

Johnson, a former leader of the Communication Workers Union himself, left it unclear which union leaders he believed were Zog-trippers and which were stay-at-homes. *Guardian* columnist Polly Toynbee addressed this deficiency in an article the same week, dividing general secretaries carefully into the 'sensible left' and 'wreckers', the latter presumably being the denizens of Zog.[1]

The focus of Johnson's complaint, echoed by Toynbee, was the criticisms of government now almost obligatory in union elections. The minister unsurprisingly failed to ask why candidates of all stripes should regard such rhetoric as essential to success. He spoke on the day that Kevin Curran was chosen as the new General Secretary of the GMB, one of the 'big four' unions which dominate the TUC. Curran made his mark by calling for a return to closed union shops (by agreement with employers), by asserting that 'some people in Number Ten do not share our values' and by declaring himself 'a great admirer of the Marxist tradition'.[2]

Curran nevertheless made Toynbee's cut as 'sensible', presumably somewhat to his embarrassment. But the whole Johnson–Toynbee offensive had served to highlight Downing Street's anxieties about union developments. The timing was not fortuitous. With the war in Iraq over and the firefighters' dispute apparently nearing its end, Tony Blair's advisers decided it was time for a counter-attack.

Yet the polemics underlined the problem ministers face. Even the 'sensible' are not sweethearts. Kevin Curran, for example, is scarcely likely to be less hostile to New Labour than his predecessor, John Edmonds. Proving that you do not have to be new to be awkward, Edmonds had been consistently critical of government policy, more so than any other union official of his stature. He ran hard-hitting advertisements attacking government handling of the public services and the firefighters' dispute. When ministers attacked this as a waste of money, the union pointed out that the advertisements had more than paid for themselves by attracting new members to the union from among the low paid, looking for an organisation to articulate their anger.

Unison's General Secretary, Dave Prentis, was also numbered among the 'sensible'. But Britain's biggest union has been a consistent, if sometimes pragmatic, thorn in the government's side. It could hardly be otherwise, since Unison's members in the public services face the consequences of the Blair–Brown privatisation project at the sharp end. Unison also takes a left-wing position on most policy issues – a particular source of unhappiness to Ms Toynbee and those of like mind. It was the first of the 'big four', for example, to affiliate to the Stop the War Coalition.

If these are the 'sensible', who needs the Zog-bound? The truth is that the whole movement is moving to the left and the leading figures in almost every major union reflect that in their specific industrial and political context. Different leaders and different unions will always respond to problems and pressures in different ways. How they synthesise their differences will be a critical factor in determining their collective success or failure in the years ahead.

Toynbee's division was, in any event, demonstrably false. Those she praised for being strictly focused on bread-and-butter issues have strong political views which they are not afraid to air. Those she dismissed as 'politicians' unconcerned with industrial matters have among the best records in terms of winning pay increases and improvements in conditions. The officials who represent the low-paid women workers of Dolphin Square, normally a prime concern of the *Guardian*'s columnist, were strong supporters, in the T&G leadership election, of the proud-to-be-awkward Tony Woodley.

Those interviewed here do not include all the union faces in the news. There is a broader changing of the guard taking place in the union movement, producing a large number of significant new leaders.

Andy Gilchrist, the much-vilified General Secretary of the Fire Brigades Union is one such. Elected to succeed the widely-respected Ken Cameron, Gilchrist has been tested as few other leaders, old or new, have been in recent years. He found himself unexpectedly cast into a full-blown confrontation with government over the union's demand for pay justice. As a consequence, Downing Street unleashed its gutter-press attack dogs onto him, using the full repertoire of anti-union tricks from earlier decades. His children were harassed, his past life raked over, he was himself demonised as a 'killer'. Whatever tactical differences emerged within the FBU in the course of the dispute, the union rallied solidly around its popular General Secretary.

It is too early to judge, at the time of writing, the longer-term consequences of this bitter dispute for either Andy Gilchrist or his union. The FBU is likely, however, to remain at the core of the left within the movement and Gilchrist's own reputation to flourish in inverse proportion to the intensity of Rupert Murdoch's attacks on him.

Paul Mackney, the leader of NATFHE, the lecturers' union, was the first of the new leaders to be elected and has, therefore, been the first to be re-elected. He was returned unopposed as General Secretary for a further five-year term in October 2002. This was remarkable insofar as NATFHE has acquired a reputation for changing its general secretary at every available opportunity since the re-election of top officials became mandatory under Thatcher-era legislation. His unopposed endorsement by the NATFHE membership is thus a further indication of the rewards to be gained by leading from the front. This Mackney has done both industrially – he has taken his members, whose pay has been eroded like so many others in the public sector, out on strike – and politically. He was one of the first union leaders to oppose the 'war on terrorism' post-September 11, and was the first union general secretary to join the platform of the Stop the War Coalition.

Jeremy Dear succeeded to the helm of the National Union of Journalists in 2002. The NUJ was long bedevilled by internal divisions, resulting in several changes in leadership and almost interminable wrangling. Under Dear, a personable left-winger, the union has taken maximum advantage of the easier climate for union recognition. More than 5000 journalists gained union protection in over 55 new recognition agreements with employers in 2001–02. 'Of course, we will always service individual members' needs, but people want more of our resources to go into promoting and supporting collective action', he says.[3]

A new leadership of the TUC itself also took over at Congress House in 2003. Brendan Barber succeeded John Monks as General Secretary with the latter leaving to run the European TUC in Brussels. Monks was almost universally admired in the trade union movement as an effective spokesman for trade unionism, a straightforward man and a highly competent administrator. His general outlook was, however, to the right of the emerging political centre of gravity in the movement.

This is not unusual for the TUC. Wherever that centre of gravity has been in the trade union movement's history, the TUC has been to the right of it. While it has sometimes been in advance of most unions in raising important questions – equality, most notably – it has been a lynch-pin of right-wing ideas on industrial relations and political strategy alike. Generally, it has worked as a force for social consensus and keeping the unions in line, rather than as a centre for organising struggle. In recent years every step forward, like the establishment of the Organising Academy to train union organisers, has been matched by a step backward, such as the setting up of a Partnership Institute to promote harmony between employers and employees. Since New Labour came to office, Congress House has divided its energies between trying to persuade ministers to deliver bits and pieces for the trade unions whilst working to ensure that the unions do nothing to upset ministers.

Maintaining this balance will be even more trying for Barber than it has been for Monks, given the low point in union–government relations reached during the firefighters' dispute, the shift to the left in the major unions and the pile-up of unresolved issues, in the public services and in relation to union law in particular. The initial indication is that Barber, a TUC employee of long standing who has never been tempted to trip to Zog, will follow the same approach as Monks, only more so.

Barber has insisted that 'the dominant model of trade union relations is now partnership'. His New Year message for 2003 emphasised his desire to build better relations with government above all. He even acknowledged that government could not always go along with union demands 'as they must govern in the interests of the whole country'. Such an attitude gives ministers their alibi for saying 'no' even before they have been asked for anything.[4]

The new General Secretary has also been keen to keep the TUC's distance from the anti-war movement. He declined all invitations to speak at the vast demonstrations organised in London in the early part of 2003, showing a scant regard for the TUC's standing with the hundreds of thousands of trade unionists who took part (or for the heavily-mobilised Muslim community, which the TUC badly needs to reach). When the TUC General Council eventually took a position critical of the government's war policy, Congress House diluted the practical implications of that dissent by proposing no follow-up action beyond a private meeting at Number Ten.

Barber's biggest difficulty, however, will be in constructing a workable coalition among union leaders for a pro-government approach, in the absence of any changes in government policy.

Barber has in turn been replaced as Deputy General Secretary of the TUC by Frances O'Grady who has the distinction of being the first woman, after nigh-on 140 years, to hold such senior office at the TUC. She served as the founding Director of the TUC's Organising

Academy and represents a more members-first approach to trade unionism, with an emphasis on campaigning. Press reports on her appointment described her as a committed socialist and feminist, which would have almost all her predecessors spinning in their graves. She was chosen for the post by the TUC executive in preference to the TUC's Head of Economics, David Coates, an outspoken advocate of social partnership with employers.

If the past is any guide to the future and the tradition of eventual promotion of the deputy to the top job continues – a procedure which has worked to the advantage of generations of male officials, deserving and not – then O'Grady will become the General Secretary of the TUC in due course. That would signal a major change in the image and the outlook of British trade unionism.

2

Bob Crow

It is a fact that the Most Hated Man in Britain has never been an employer. 'Most Hated Man in Britain' is a title strictly reserved by the tabloid media for leading trade unionists. Probably the first to be officially so dubbed, although certainly not the first to be vilified, was Charlie Doyle, a Communist power worker and strike leader in London in the 1950s. At various times, the laurel has passed to Mick McGahey, Ray Buckton, Arthur Scargill and, in one Sun newspaper sally, Communist Party industrial organiser Mick Costello.

For a time in the 1990s the title was retired. Perhaps some synthetic celebrity hate-figures briefly aspired, but it just was not the same. Today, however, we have a clear front-runner: Bob Crow, General Secretary of the Rail Maritime and Transport Union (RMT), the largest union in the railway industry.

You might have been forgiven for thinking that the privatised railway industry might have produced a few reasonable contenders for the Most Hated Man title from the employers' side, after six years of catastrophes, incompetence and buck-passing, lubricated by unabashed greed – but the job is one of those few for which Trade Unionists Only may apply.

The average newspaper reader has been given an alarming image of Crow over the last year or two – Millwall supporter (nobody likes us, we don't care, etc.), son of an East End dockworker, strike-happy, far-left and so on. He has been made to fit the bill for Daily Mail nightmares. The Evening Standard has led the press pack in his pursuit, sending reporters to follow Crow around at weekends and helpfully advising readers how he travels to work.

It's not particularly funny. On New Year's morning 2002 he was attacked by two men on his doorstep, one of whom smashed him in the face with an iron bar. They seemed intent on maximum personal violence rather than robbery. Bob Crow himself believes they may have had some connection with renegade employers. Whatever the truth of this may be, RMT members – workers who have borne the brunt of the railway privatisation catastrophe – elected him their new General Secretary by an enormous margin just a few months later. They like him, no doubt, because he appears to care about the things they care about themselves.

Have the police got anywhere in finding your attackers?
No, nothing. They've put a panic button in my house and put a couple of yellow boards up in the area. Never heard another word. They might have taken it more seriously if I had been Princess Di's butler.

Does the vilification bother you?
I have been trained to believe that if the media attack you, you must be doing something right. Of course, they try and make a personality out of you – nice guys don't sell newspapers, so they're going to try to demonise you.

But I do object to what the *Evening Standard* has been doing, saying we are going to follow you and we can make it easy or make it hard, and then talk to my fifteen-year-old son about his parents' activities. I don't mind it personally, but not for my kid.

I used to be demonised about twice a year, now it seems like every day. But I put up with it. I remember an old CPer telling me that Keir Hardie said that 'when the capitalist press praise me, I know I have done wrong to my fellow man'.

Do you feel part of a big change in the movement?
Without a doubt there has been a change from where we were ten years ago. Then it was 'we don't like what's going on, but there's nothing we can do', everyone was very apathetic. Now we feel we can do things. That does not just mean strike action or revolutionary phrase-mongering, but that people are more confident than they were in the dismal years. They gave Labour the benefit of the doubt for four years. Now they want real change.

People feel let down by Labour, they don't want another kind of Tory government. They want jobs, housing, decent education for their kids, something done about drugs and the Labour government is not delivering it.

The trade union movement is on the move, no doubt about it, although it is not what it was in the 1970s in terms of numbers, not by any stretch of the imagination. What is emerging more and more is that there is a confidence in people to fight for better conditions. There's not the same amount of slagging off of trade union leaders.

There's new leaders …
There's Mick Rix, Jeremy Dear, Paul Mackney, Billy [*Hayes*], Andy [*Gilchrist*]. They've all been elected, so it's not just a fluke vote. People want a campaigning fighting lead. That's what I'm trying to do – we've got the best relationship we've had with ASLEF for twenty-five years,

officials are working together better than ever before, it all comes from more confidence.

Could this lead to a change in the Labour Party?
I do not say that one particular party should have the exclusive rights to socialism. There are some very good people left in the Labour Party – the Campaign Group of MPs, RMT's own campaign group, people of my point of view. But it's the very opposite if you go to the Labour Party conference. People say you can fight from within, but how do you do that when you see the way the conference is rigged? It has to be changed back to being a resolution-based conference. It is a party that is pro-capitalist.

But if the unions can change, can't they change the Party too?
I suppose it is possible to turn it around. But it would be a hell of a job. Like it or not, the Party was hijacked by 'New Labour', although it's not new, it's old-fashioned class collaboration. It's a situation where the Liberals are to the left of Labour in the main now. It's very, very difficult to support a party that is bombing Iraq and Afghanistan and taking on the firefighters [*the day of the interview, Tony Blair had pledged to crush the 'Scargillite' Fire Brigades Union*].

But trade unions need to do something politically ...
Trade union politics are never going to be enough. As Lenin said, trade union politics are bourgeois politics. You can get a shorter working week, better pay, better pensions, more holidays and then ten years later you can lose it all again. You need a fundamental shift for working people, which can only be done on a fundamental basis, a change from capitalism to socialism.

You need a party to fight on behalf of working people – there is a massive vacuum there. The Tories are still there, in the final analysis still working for the ruling class, Labour and Liberals. There is a big gap, the representation of working people. You can never say never, or we would have stuck with the Liberals 102 years ago.

I think we have to work on the issues first of all – public ownership, the repeal of the anti-union laws, end PPP on the tube, Europe – build broad movements on these. At some point people are going to have to make a judgement as to how we are going to get something different.

Are we going to see a return of the railways to public ownership?
We are not going to get it from the present government which is happy to put billions into private companies. We have a Labour government privatising the Underground which is a step backwards from public ownership. They call it something different, but more than six thousand workers are going to be working for private companies. It's disgusting. This government is not going to do anything for public ownership. It's privatising things the Tories never did.

What does socialism mean to you now?
Well, we're a long way away from it. In a socialist society you would have jobs, decent housing, a decent NHS, education, living in a world of peace. Capitalist society is never going to do those things – capitalism can't do without the unemployed, it can't do without wars, can't build new homes.

It suits capitalism to have a division among workers, with them digging into each other. I work for socialism, but I also have to work in the situation as it is, you have to bargain in the world as it is.

What influenced your own views?

My father's docks and trade union background played a key part in forming my approach to life and politics. Socialism and trade unionism were drummed into me from an early age. The Communist Party also had a massive influence, providing all my political understanding – it was a university education on its own.

You have been very strongly against the Euro.

If you don't control your currency you can't control your own fiscal policy and therefore you are no longer a government.

Are you making progress in tackling equality issues in RMT?

Equalities issues are not just about having black, women's and gay and lesbian committees for the sake of them, but trying to open up the union's structures as widely as possible with the aim of involving the widest possible range of members. It's about ensuring that the union pursues the interests of all its members.

You've been very outspoken against the war on Iraq. Do RMT members support this?

I always speak my mind. People either accept it or they don't.

3

Heather Wakefield

If the tabloid-designated 'awkward squad' is the future of trade unionism, then in one sense the future does resemble the past – it is male and white. Obviously no crime in an individual, it is a condition which could be ruinous to the trade union movement as a whole. With more than half the workforce in Britain now women, trade unions have nowhere to grow if they do not come to reflect this reality. Some progress has been made over the last generation, but it falls far short of the standards demanded. Trade union leaderships still do not look like the people they aim to represent – male, pale and too often stale remains the rule.

Heather Wakefield is the national officer of Unison responsible for local government and one of the leaders of the strike by municipal employees in 2002, amongst other things the largest strike by women workers in Britain's history. She does not fit into comfortable stereotypes, and not only because she is pale but neither male nor stale. Her route into trade unionism lay through community activism more than workplace conflict, her outlook informed more by a holistic sense of how working-class women live than by a narrowly-focused concept of class. Yes, the personal and the public intertwine more explicitly, too: her children are a repeated point of reference, and when she searches for some criteria to evaluate a new problem she speculates as to what the opinion of her late Aunt

Dorothy might have been, rather than the lads in the branch room or the oft-invoked judgement of 'history'. And she is probably the only national trade union official to have met Barry White and Elton John in the course of her working life.

How did you come into trade unionism?
My first union was the NUJ [*National Union of Journalists*]. I had been features editor of the Student Union magazine in Reading and I wanted to work as a journalist. There was a magazine called *Beat Instrumental*, started in the 1960s by the same guy who ran the Beatles Fan Club magazine. I sent them an article about David Bowie so they offered me a job. I interviewed Joan Armatrading, Barry White, The Who and Elton John. It was a horrible time for music. The Bay City Rollers were big then. Then I became a trainee social worker in Newham and joined NALGO and became branch publicity officer.

I went to work in Lewisham, working on women's employment in Docklands. I was in NUPE and became the President of Lewisham and Deptford Trades Council. This was in 1980 – it was pretty blokey then, lots of men from the print and craft unions. They were older, mostly CP or ex-CPers, and then there were these younger public sector people. That was when a private/public sector split started to emerge around the cuts.

I remember a couple of print workers turning up at the Trades Council in beautiful suits and shirts, obviously having just had a dinner cooked by wifey back at home, and there was I straight from work eating chips from a bag and they told me off for showing disrespect to the Trades Council. But most of the old guard were very supportive and they recognised that things had to change. I tried to bring what was happening to women's employment into the Trades Council. I was working on equal pay, working with local unions and working on unionisation with Frances [*O'Grady, now TUC Deputy General Secretary*].

What sort of image did the women you were working with have of trade unionism?
A lot of them were just bemused. It was interesting. In Deptford, you had the docks, a strong T&G tradition, there was also a very significant amount of casualised labour around the fur trade and food manufacturing. We were able to link recruitment with a lot of other activities, like oral history, getting women to talk. We saw trade unionism in terms of a much bigger picture, it was one dimension, not capable of capturing all of their concerns at that time.

And there was a real fear of shark employers around. Quite a lot of the women came from families with male trade unionists, so they were not at all hostile, but they regarded it as strange – why me, why would I want to join, what could it add to my life?

That was twenty years ago. Could unions capture all those concerns now?
I feel very unsure about how to answer that. Obviously, trade unions have taken on a lot of issues, like child care, sexual harassment or domestic violence. In Newham we did a project on women's health, which went down like hot cakes. Women do feel more comfortable about bringing up some of the big things that affect them.

The difficulties are becoming more disguised. The nature of domestic labour, what goes on in homes and how it affects women's lives – it is fundamental to existing power relations and power structures, it is difficult to describe – it is the structure of women's self-confidence and self-image. The Estelle [*Morris, who had just resigned as Education Secretary saying she was 'not up to it'*] factor has brought this to the fore. Hopefully, there will be more of a debate.

Women's economic power is still weak· because of unequal pay. Women still generally earn less. Even though only 15 per cent of households are now two parents with children, the 1950s notion of a male bread-winner is still fixed. It underpins that pay structure in local government and the public sector of the economy. Catering, cleaning, caring work, all the things that women do in the home are hugely under-valued in the labour market.

How do you address that self-image issue?
Trade unions could do it by example, but the fact is that union officialdom is still generally male-dominated, particularly at the top. Few of the unions take succession planning seriously, getting women into key positions.

Because most of the men have been around in the same unions for a long time, there are seldom women who have comparable experience. I remember sitting in a room with four senior union members with over 130 years' experience between them.

Would that have felt different if you were a younger man with similar experience?
Probably it would have felt different if I was a man. I think women set themselves very high standards, which is why they are more prone to get ME, for example. Women are interpreted completely differently. If they are ambitious they are pushy, while in men it is valued and welcomed.

Unions do not value the other experiences enough – organising in the community, in the women's movement, in campaigning on issues for children or equal pay – they don't count because they are not as good as having dealt with the bonus scheme.

How did you get into negotiating yourself?
I did consider applying for a full-time job with the union in the

mid-1980s. I noticed a vacancy for a regional officer of NUPE just around the time that I had my first kid and at the time I was with an official trying to organise crèches for workers in local colleges and he said I should not consider applying because, he said, I could never do it with a small child, because I would be having to go to evening meetings. I did not pursue it at the time because I had my doubts ...

What would you say now if an official was to say that to someone in similar circumstances?

I would say, first, that it is a complete myth that you have to spend evenings out – it is more a matter of going down the pub with the branch secretary and you can easily organise your working life around children and domestic commitments. It was complete bollocks. I don't think any official would say it like that now – some might think it though.

Anyway I got a job in the NUPE research department down in Woolwich at the time, doing equality stuff, health service pay, doing an equality audit of agreements.

I was in the research department until 1992, when I had Miya, my second child. I applied to be a regional official, having cracked that it was a bit of a doddle. I wanted to get negotiating experience. In 1996 I became a national negotiating officer for local government, then three years ago deputy head and now I am temporary head.

So you had a different background – what did that help you bring to union negotiating?

Some 75 per cent of local government workers are women. It has given me an understanding as to how to put the pieces of the jigsaw together. You understand how sexual harassment affects women's daily lives, how domestic circumstances constrain their lives. Maternity rights, equal pay campaigns outside the union have operated differently, campaigning conduct too.

How?
Women get more fun – much more having a laugh. It came to the fore in the [*local government*] dispute. I remember on the picket line in Newcastle women chucking fifteen penny coins in the air, because that was how much the increase was worth to them. There is a social dimension – having a laugh at blokes a lot of the time.

So is there a difference in how solidarity is expressed? In more traditional, male trade unionism it is almost a physical solidarity, reflecting joint manual work and the picket line …
It reflects women's jobs. Wiping bums in residential homes, clearing up dribble and sick, or looking after very sick babies, you develop ways of coping, you see human existence at its lowest ebb. It's like all oppressed people, there is no aspect of life that is hidden. Women have a brilliant way of turning that into humour. Compassion, it's just kind of there, it is very hard to define.

My mum was a school cleaner all through my childhood, first at the local girls' convent school, the one that Marianne Faithfull went to – I went to see her in the school play that launched her career! I remember my mum's dedication to that job – stripping and polishing the school hall in the summer holidays, making sure she did it perfectly for the kids, so they had something nice when they came back to school. There was a connection between that kind of work and what went on in the school. Now it has been reduced to a series of manual tasks to be done as quickly as possible, they have knocked all the human dimension out of it. There is much more hidden in that kind of job – she was always getting students out of scrapes. But she had very low expectations of her pay.

You have mentioned oppression as something distinct from exploitation. How does that shape what trade unions should do?

Using the word is hopeless. It has got to be unpicked. A lot of men do not understand that they are oppressive. You say they are a pain in the arse and they are taken aback. If you have been around for twenty-five years you do not think anyone can do the job better than you, you have no self-doubt at all.

Oppression manifests itself in small daily things, not a jackboot coming down; in a reluctance by men to change their behaviour or relinquish their power. I remember a few years ago Frances being told by a man at her work, after a disagreement, that he did not 'like her body language' and by coincidence a few days later I had a similar argument and the man told me that 'moodwise I was completely wrong' and I had been destructive. It really brought home the ways in which men empower and the techniques they have for keeping women in their place. They say they are changing, but they will not let you challenge them in a fundamental sense.

If it's that difficult in trade unions, which are better than most employers, how do you empower women trade unionists in their workplaces?

I do not think that trade unions are better. There are lots of private sector employers where Human Resource Management has been completely overhauled, but it's not happened within trade unions. I think there needs to be an open debate within trade unions about sexism, about wanting women to hold positions and about why it has not happened. At the moment there is almost a retreat from having that debate. A lot of the blokes are very defensive about it – it is getting worse.

All the new leaders are men. Unions have got to set some very clear targets, about what sort of organisation they want to be. It is about recognising that women need to be at the top of the unions and that their experience needs to be put in the organising strategy, creating a structure that allows for that kind of dialogue. There is an incredibly narrow and traditional lifestyle of men at the top of the unions, which does not recognise the diversity of human experience. Trade unions cannot succeed unless they change.

The media talk of going back to the 1970s with the awkward squad, but that's not possible …
The people you need to recruit, they are deeply turned off by big white tough blokes – Phil Mitchell style trade unions – that is what people see. Women are completely turned off, it is alienating and irrelevant. They say 'where do I fit in with that?' The tough boy image means women will expect from the trade union movement the same as they get in the home and who wants that?

There are a lot of blokes who have been thinking hard about how they relate to women in their lives in general, but there is nothing about them [*the 'awkward squad'*] that is saying that they realise that there is a problem. I see all this from the point of view of my mum and my Aunt Dorothy. How do you deal with it? A bunch of all white men as the image of trade unions – it does not change the power structure within unions or empower women.

Is Unison any better?
Some 71 per cent of Unison members are women. There are three

women out of twelve regional secretaries and three women among
the senior negotiating officials here [*head office*]. But the power-house
is still all boys, four men on the same floor, all very comfortable in
each other's company ...

bonded ...

... super-glued. Women are outside of the day-to-day decision-making.
We deal with the bread-and-butter stuff. But it has got a bit better
since Dave [*Prentis*] became General Secretary. He is more aware of
the importance of gender difference.

There are reserved seats for women on the National Executive, but
it does not reflect the gender composition of our membership. That
is what we tried to rectify in the dispute ...

What was the background to the local government strike?

The media was dying to reproduce the winter of discontent – pile up
the binbags. The media would have loved it, the public wouldn't, and
it would not have highlighted the real issue of the low paid.

In some ways it was an officer-led dispute. It was an ambitious
claim, and there was a bit of concern among the lay members. We
decided we would highlight those groups of women who were
low paid, not fall into the trap of trying to recreate the 'winter of
discontent'. There were lots of discussions in our local government
committee and a lot of resistance to not doing it in the traditional way
with an all-out strike by refuse workers. There was also a shift in the
union thinking to how we position ourselves as a public service union,
how we get across the message about who local government workers
are, what they do. We wanted to get the users of the service with us.
We produced leaflets aimed at the public right from the start to get

across our case, used local newspapers to explain why we were on strike, how low pay would lead to a recruitment crisis and so on.

So we developed a press strategy around that. Once we started, women just piled in. There was a woosh of anger from teachers' assistants. It was like they had been given permission. Most of them were from NUPE, where there was no notion of lay membership leadership. It was traditionally very paternalistic, male officers talking about 'my ladies' and 'yes, girls, I know what's best for you'.

The lid had been kept on for so long. It just blew off. Women began to redefine themselves and redefine their union as a women's union.

So that's very important, it takes industrial action against employers to start getting some of the changes in unions themselves that you'd been talking about … I am sure there are other ways but there are very few areas in every-day trade unions in which women can feel free to express anger and frustration at their pay and conditions. The challenge is to maintain that kind of momentum. It is now manifesting itself in small but interesting ways – in committee elections, women becoming much more vocal.

There were a lot of pissed off women because the settlement was good for the lowest paid, but not so good for those not on the very bottom of the pay structure. There had been a sense of euphoria, then disappointment. People wanted more industrial action, but we could not have won it with a series of one-day actions. It was a struggle to get a critical mass of selective action. Because there had not been a national strike since 1989, most people involved had never been involved in industrial action before. We were always very clear that the objective of the action was to get the employer back to the negotiating table.

But I don't know how else you do it. Most [*Unison*] branches are male-dominated and they are increasingly white-collar dominated. There is a class issue within the branches, although it is unpopular to say so. You need a grass-roots workplace organisation if you are to create a climate in which concerns and anger can be expressed. If that kind of attitude was harnessed at local level, in branch activities, it would be a completely different union – re-engaging with the grass-roots membership, what we used to call the rank and file.

I was interested that in your article in the Guardian *about the dispute you wrote that what you called 'Very Old Labour' councillors had been the worst* ...[5]
Mostly from the North, from some of the almost rotten boroughs. There is an old Labour hegemony in those northern councils which is very paternalistic and dreadful towards their workforce. Of course, they are often rooted in unions themselves, and they have the same attitude to 'their girlies' and 'our ladies' and really feel that a woman's place is in the home, and they take the same point of view as employers. They think that women are basically earning enough already.

The pressure to privatise and compete in the market in basic traditional services, that New Labour pressure, added to a kind of sense of outrage that their positions of power as politicians might be challenged by bloody women ... they could not believe it.

So sexism and New Labour privatisation and policies come together ...
It is a lethal cocktail. You have councils that are incredibly strapped for cash, with PFI and so on pushing councils down the road of market testing and competition, with all those blokes who do not believe women are worth much more money anyway. One of the problems is a big shift towards privatising women's jobs to save money.

Did you see that Digby Jones of the CBI had said that cutting pay levels was the whole point of PFI, and that it could not work without it. The main unions, Unison, T&G, GMB, have been anti-PFI but still saying pay cuts can somehow be avoided …

Unison has always been very anti-PFI, and it's not been until this year that we got the other unions on board. We are campaigning hard against it, but we do whatever we can to protect our members and prevent the development of a two-tier workforce. That is absolutely right, and there have been big steps forward. That is the real politics.

So do you think unions are on the way back?

I think what is happening is that trade unions are becoming the focus of people's legitimate frustrations with the government and what is clear is that the leaders of a number of unions, that is the 'awkward squad' are prepared to be overtly oppositional. That is new.

In other ways we are going backwards. I do not feel that the public portrayal of unions is going to persuade people to join. People generally want a good relationship with their employer. They want strong leadership if there is a problem, but I just do not think that is what is going on now. They do not want just militancy for its own sake.

Well, Bob Crow for example is very popular with his members because he is giving a strong lead after they have had years of being kicked around.

There are different ways of giving an impression of strength. You are not going to recruit the young, the part-time, temporary workers – are they going to think that that is for me?

I just wonder what my mum and Aunt Dorothy would think … neither of them are here now.

What did Aunt Dorothy do?
She was a cleaner, and worked in catering. She was a very thoughtful woman.

That's one generation, what about the next?
My son is very big on anti-globalisation politics. But he's like – oh, not Phil Mitchell again. He thinks about gender politics, but he asks me, do you work with these people, is that what they're like? He thinks it is really old-fashioned stuff.

You have to make trade unions a part of the same civic society. You cannot do it all just by industrial action.

4

Derek Simpson

Sir Ken Jackson rejoiced in the title of 'Tony Blair's favourite trade unionist'. It is most unlikely that this title will ever be bestowed on Derek Simpson. It is absolutely certain that he is not seeking it. He can, however, claim to be more popular than 'Tony Blair's favourite trade unionist'. His narrow victory over Sir Ken in July 2002 – four recounts, less than a thousand votes in it out of nearly 170,000 cast – convinced all but the most sceptical that there was something new afoot in the trade union movement.

amicus, the union Simpson now leads, is the product of multiple mergers. Simpson rose through the AEEU wing, which united the old Amalgamated Engineering Union (AEU), which had traditionally been right-wing, with the exception of the 1970s interlude of the presidency of Hugh Scanlon, and the former electricians' union, the EETPU. The latter had been in the grip of an even more right-wing group since the early 1960s. Frank Chapple and Eric Hammond were among Sir Ken Jackson's predecessors as its leader. This prolonged right-wing rule was the background to Sir Ken's evident astonishment at his defeat. The AEEU's partner in the 2002 merger which created amicus is MSF (Manufacturing Science Finance). MSF brought together ASTMS, led for many years by the trade union movement's pioneering bon viveur *Clive Jenkins, and*

TASS, headed by Ken Gill. Simpson shares the leadership of the merged union, the TUC's second biggest affiliate, with Roger Lyons, briefly celebrated for having claimed a 25 pence currant bun on union expenses.

Derek Simpson himself was a regional official of the AEEU before he decided to risk his job (he had to resign his full-time position) by standing for election against Sir Ken, who had initially hoped to extend his term of office for two years past his retirement age of sixty-five without troubling the members with an election. He now heads a union with strong democratic traditions but an officialdom largely raised in the spirit of 'social partnership'. Adversity has left Simpson dryly humorous.

When I asked them if they thought trade unionism was reviving, both Jack Jones and Ken Gill immediately identified your election as the most important positive sign that things were changing.

I don't think that the movement ever went away. I think it has been a question of heads down and the people like New Labour and their trade union equivalents who have been in the ascendancy because militants and progressives have been hounded. We have lost a generation, the Thatcher years, not only in the sense of young people never being in the unions, but living through a period where the unions were vigorously attacked by government and where the long-established companies and industries which were the bedrock of trade unions, their activists and their leaders, were gone.

I would see that as the root of a lot of the problems that trade unions have got now. Unions do not exist as benevolent, friendly societies that you want to be a member of in a charitable sense, like the Women's Institute. There are problems at work and our collective ability to tackle those problems is why unions exist. That has never gone away and arguably the trauma of the Thatcher years has heightened the need for trade unions. People should have been flooding into the trade unions, but because all this took place against a background of a massive decline in our manufacturing base, the whole question took on a different perspective. People were either long-term unemployed, non-working class or they were just grateful for owt they could have in a culture where there is so much diversion and distraction. Even in poverty people were able to smoke, drink, have TVs and people had the ability to go out, youngsters went to dances … so many distractions in life. But the problems still exist for all that.

What is interesting to me is that some of the unions which have been growing are not the ones with the great traditions. The civil service union elected Mark Serwotka, Paul Mackney at [NATFHE], Billy Hayes at the communications workers. These people have been winning elections in unions which do not have a militant tradition. I see that as an indication that even in these areas there is a growing sense of the need for trade unions. The only reason why a lot of the classic trade unions have not emerged more strongly is because of the problems in industry. It's still going on now, week after week, redundancies here, closures there. It's not conducive to building numbers.

But perhaps Ken Gill and Jack Jones have identified something. My union has never been noted for producing left-wing leaders. I am probably the most left-wing leader that has ever been elected. I don't actually think that even Scanlon would come into my category. I did it against the machine, and it showed what the feelings were among the rank and file.

But none of this changes the problems in industry. The only thing is that the trade unions could not be destroyed by the Tory attacks because of the scale of the problems for working people that were created. The Tories were not tackling the problems, they were attacking the solution, which was the unions, and the problems have not gone away. I am still facing those problems and the Tories didn't change them.

Your election literature spoke about 'the demand for change and the feeling that it is long overdue' among members of the AEU. How is that being expressed?

Somebody once said to me, and it stuck, that 'the problem people have is that before finding answers you have to understand the question'. It's like they have in exam papers – 'please read the question carefully before starting your answer'. One of the problems we have … it's difficult because there are many layers to it, and if I give you just one layer you'll have to take it on trust that I have other points as well …

New Labour, Blair and all the rest of them, surfaced at a time when the labour movement was down, when the Tories appeared invincible, after the fourth election defeat. The modernisers said they would change things. You certainly have to give them credit for their timing, because by the time the next election came along, I believe anyone could have beaten the Tories. They said the only way to win was to adopt the New Labour model, and now it looks like the successes were down to New Labour and everything before it was crap.

New Labour is going to get thrashed, completely destroyed, with its ideology, when the Tories or some other opposition finally gets its act together and then the argument that you can't win without New Labour will disappear.

New Labour, third way, partnership, to me it is all the Emperor's clothes. At the time when everybody wanted to beat the Tories, we all said how wonderful it was but now people are thinking to themselves, he's got nothing on …

Are you the little boy who says so?

It comes back to understanding the question. Nobody is asking the question yet, but everybody is saying, he's not wearing nowt, but they daren't say so out loud. We have got to say 'what a wonderful suit it is' but nobody dare say the truth. One of the things New Labour has done in the labour movement is to make it harder to find opportunities to say so. It's like what [*Sir Ken*] Jackson was doing here, putting officers in, ruthlessly doing a job. New Labour has been busy filling parliament full of Blair clones, centralised control, working to exterminate any kind of opposition.

But as soon as somebody comes clean and says Blair isn't wearing anything then the whole thing will collapse like a pack of cards. So the people out there aren't asking me to just change anything, but to ask the question they want to have asked, then they'll say 'that's right, let's do something about it'. Probably I am in a position to ask the question at the moment, it's just stupid that it only has to be me – not because I am more articulate or clever than anybody else.

And I am going to ask the question. I resigned my job to stand in the election, I don't want a knighthood or to go to the House of Lords. I am only here to fight for the underdog and my only ambition is to serve working people.

What is worrying the establishment is not just the vote I got, which was a narrow win, but the whole campaign I fought. It was against the machine, all the full-time officers, the union establishment, history and all the union journals. I had to fight against all of that and I won. My votes were passionate votes, votes from the heart. His votes were votes for loyalty, for the machine.

Now I have got that support and I have got the machine as well. What can I now do with the full resources of the union behind me?

I could take anyone on. Number Ten must be cringing because I have not just got the grass-roots support, I have got the machine as well and I can say and do things. And I am going to be the voice that asks the question – where are the Emperor's clothes?

When did you decide to challenge Sir Ken? It seemed to people outside the union a bit like you were tilting at windmills.

It didn't start off with challenging Sir Ken. Deciding to challenge the electricians for control of the union was the first decision, when it was thought that Sir Ken would be retiring in March of this year [*2002*]. We were expecting that there would be an election for a replacement, that he would be retiring and that one of the full-time officials on the Executive Committee would be a candidate.

I started thinking that we have to have a go at challenging it. People laughed for the obvious reasons, they laughed that it might be me because I did not have a high profile.

Then Jackson decided he would stay on without fighting an election. I challenged that, sought a legal opinion and that having been won I would force him to retire. So he changed the rules to allow him to stay on, but it forced him into an election. Then I had to resign my job to stand against him. I felt that things were getting so bad that somebody had to. It was destroying the union. He was systematically turfing out democratic elements, replacing them with a rigid, centralised, controlling bureaucracy and you could see the union going down the pan.

Nothing I have learned since my election has suggested I was wrong. It was very much the case that people were ruthlessly grabbing control of the union and milking it to their own advantage financially.

Can you put a stop to that?
[*a very long pause followed by a sigh*] If I can correct some of the wrongs that have been done, put right years of damage to the structure, put back the pride in what was a jewel in the movement, but is now seen as a pariah … we have been undermining other unions, undercutting them, not to the benefit of our members, but just to the detriment of others.

So is rebuilding relationships with other trade unions a priority?
Yes. One of the things that will make a difference is that I will be proud to work in unity. I will not be signing any more no-strike deals, I will not be setting out to undercut other unions. And where those deals which we have signed in the past are not working, I will be proud to rip up those agreements and look at them again from scratch. And I am asking other unions not to step over me and take advantage, because what I am doing is in everybody's interest. We want to lift the base of trade union agreements. Instead of competing to sign the lowest deal, offering employers the most, we want to be competing to sign the best deal for members. We don't want to lower the base line, we are setting out to raise it. If you like, we are cutting out the low-cost supplier in the trade union market. We want a choice of British Airways, without competition from Easyjet and the like in terms of trade unionism.

How is scrapping no-strike deals going down?
Where our members want to change their agreements they can, is what I'm saying. Many of them are crap – these are not agreements made by them, but over their heads by the union. In some of them you can't even negotiate on wages. People say, what should I be in a

trade union for, why should I stop in the union when you do not even negotiate my wages? There are hundreds of examples.

I'm saying you can put it to a vote. If you want to rip it up, you can. But there is no point in going around arguing about it, if you want to put up with a bad agreement, I'm not going to argue about it. As far as I am concerned we need to be signing agreements that give something. Trade union recognition is not an end in itself, it is a means to an end – better wages and conditions. We need agreements that lead to those ends.

Is this an end to social partnership?
I said that at the TUC, and it caused a bit of an upset. The Japanese car companies have had a meeting to decide what to do about that. We are finding that union officers are being invited to things for the first time in years. Nissan invited Davy Hall [*AEEU official in north-east*] to the launch of a new car, and that's the first time ever, and we've had an agreement with them since the 1980s! They know that something has been said, they are aware it will make demands on them.

But in a sense social partnership is not finished – it's finished only in the sense of being something beyond what already existed, which is normal negotiation. We've always had partnerships – you sit down and negotiate wages. The gaffer says he wants to do this, and he wants us to do that. He talks about suppliers and plants and making that cheaper, about incentives and in the end you come out with something you agree about, and that is collective bargaining.

Now they want to put another name on it and it becomes a woolly word. It means something else, and it means that what was taking place already, what has always been taking place, wasn't partnership, it was something else all of a sudden. What does it all come down to – he wants to make a profit, we want more wages. That is what I mean by partnership. It's as if everything that we were doing before is now wrong and we have to find a new way of doing it called 'partnership'.

What I do is collective bargaining, where you go to the employer and say we're in a boat, we know where we want to go to, we're rowing and you're steering …

Don't you think we could do the steering as well as the rowing?
Well, that should be the case but I've not finished the point I'm making. What we've had is partnership but it was never called by that word. Now we're told partnership is against a backcloth of New Labour saying everything in the past was bad and now we've got to try something different, it actually becomes 'anti-partnership'. We had partnership, it wasn't right, we now have something new called 'partnership', so it becomes an anti-partnership …

An anti-partnership where you do not discuss wages, conditions, it's all customers first, suppress whatever the workers want, all their problems and concerns, do it my way because I know how to make the business succeed. That is not partnership. It is the employer saying give me what I want and you can have what's left over. It is suppressing my interests and putting the proceeds directly into employers' pockets. It is destroying what the real partnership was.

What we should be organising is a true partnership, a partnership of equals. That is the TUC position. They say that. Why talk about 'true partnership'? It means that what we have at the moment is not true partnership. They can't say that – they are still saying 'what a nice suit' but we are saying 'he's stark bollock naked', so the TUC says 'we believe in *true* sartorial elegance'.

Partnership – it's all smoke and mirrors.

Can this new union attitude be carried into the Labour Party itself?
Spin doctors are trying to destroy rank-and-file democracy in favour of centralised power and control. The real agenda is to find a way of doing away with the Labour–trade union link. The biggest threat to the New Labour myth is the trade union movement. If it kicks into gear it can mobilise its troops, its finances, its block votes to bring down New Labour internally, that is within the Party. So they want to marginalise trade unions – that is their biggest threat. Trade union unity is the answer. It is about basic principles, exposing the third way and New Labour.

What are those basic principles?
I think we have to show the contradictions. If you want to attack someone, the clever way to do it is not to start off by attacking them. Like, if you're doing this interview you don't start an argument with me because you know I won't say what you want, but you say 'yes, yes' even if you're secretly thinking I'm a wanker because you want me to carry on …

Actually I really do agree with you.
But you'd say so anyway. You need to get them to drive their argument to the point of collapse. There's a mathematical technique called *reductio … ad absurdum*: driving the argument to the point where it collapses under its own contradiction, it destroys itself as illogical. We should reduce New Labour arguments to the point of being ridiculous. I'll give a simple example – flexible workforce.

People say 'flexible workforce, what's that?' What does it mean? Does it mean somebody who is multi-skilled, who can move from job to job? Or someone who works through an agency, has no rights, low wages, no pension and is a cheap and reliable source of labour? A workforce that is unestablished, eager-to-please, embraces new technology and so on, so the government can say, 'it's safe here, you can build your factory here'. The philosophy is that we will have inward investment, making jobs and prosperity and ending unemployment.

Two things are wrong here. There is a flexible labour force in India, Pakistan, China, but it has not brought them economic prosperity. It's a load of bollocks. It has meant maximum profit for employers but no end to the economic problems for the people.

Second, a flexible workforce means it is as easy for them to leave as it is for them to come. One of the things that contributes to a flexible workforce is that we have the lowest level of employment standards in Europe. We don't adopt European standards, we work to dilute them. The disadvantage is that when an employer decides on a rationalisation and reorganisation and wants to solve their economic problems and losses, it is easier for them to make job cuts here.

So what happens is that we lose the high-paid, high-skilled jobs in well-established firms and get the low-paid simple jobs. Because we have no way of resisting the employers if they want to come and go.

Like Dyson, they shut production down here and take the jobs around the world and still want to sell their goods here.

What should be done about that?
We should not be buying Dyson's fucking Hoovers. We should put an income barrier on them so nobody would want to buy them because they are too expensive. We should tell them to go back and sell them in China, if that's where they are now making them. I would say, if you want to sell them here, make them here. If not, we should tell them to fuck off. I know people will say it means trade barriers ...

It would mean a radical change in the world capitalist economy ...

It is radical in the sense that people in management have to show some commitment to their workforce. We don't even ask the question. If I suggested this to Blair he would look at me like I'm gone out. He would say that that is outrageous, but if you ask most people they don't think that it is outrageous at all. People at meetings don't see it like that at all. Most people see the point.

It exposes this philosophy of the third way, the flexible workforce, shows what it is all about. Mention flexible workforce and people say 'yeah', but if you say it means working for whatever people want to pay you, doing whatever they want, not saying boo to a goose, whether the job is pleasant or not, and you cannot opt out of it because you won't get any benefit, they see it differently.

It's like the cattle market. You are not allowed to say, 'I just want to stay out here and graze' – I just want enough to eat, simple life, I don't want anything fancy. No, they herd you, they say you have to go to market, you run here, you run there, you have no say which channel you are herded into, it's someone saying 'you this way, you that way'.

Someone has got to raise these questions, got to ask them. People sometimes just raise it from the point of view of how it affects *them*. Particular unions raise it in terms of how it affects *them* and their own wages. Where the difference is now is that people are beginning to ask the question in a way that is casting doubt, and pressure will be piled on us to kill that ideology.

Are you prepared for that pressure?

I'm not saying that they will be able to kill it. I don't think they can. If I could be completely neutralised, sent to an island, or bumped off that wouldn't be the end of it. The new mood comes from what is happening out there, from the things that people are confronting. I am just describing it. If the third way actually did work, and I was saying it was rubbish, no one would listen to me.

I remember once I was speaking at a meeting, and I was slagging off the bosses, saying they had big cars, expense accounts and so on, and some guy at the back shouted at me 'you're a fucking hypocrite, fuck off to Russia'. I asked what he meant and he said 'if you won the pools tomorrow, you would live like that'. I said 'That's absolutely right. If I won the pools tomorrow, I would live like that. And tomorrow you would still be coming into work in this shithole, for crap wages and nothing else would have changed in the world, you daft bastard.' End of argument. That was nearly thirty-five years ago.

But what you say has to match reality. You can hold a meeting and say there hasn't been a massacre, you can pass a resolution saying there was no massacre, but if you then come out of the hall and there are bodies everywhere it stops being a matter for debate.

That is why the government can't beat underlying trade union principles, because they can't deal with the problems that are there. You can fool some of the people some of the time, but the issues keep coming back. People are now asking the questions, awaking from a sleep, rousing from their slumbers, waking up to smell the coffee – just like they did with Thatcher. The people who thought she was wonderful ended up wanting to hang her from a gas lamp because she had told them a pack of lies. That's why Blair's popularity is suffering. He has told 'em this and told 'em that but it is not what their own life experiences are telling them.

So you have the votes, the conviction, and now you've got the machine and you've got seven years. What are you going to do with it, where would you like to be at the end of those seven years?

I would like to see trade union membership grow. I would like to see this union grow – I would like to see further amalgamations, I'm sure we could be the biggest union in the country again. I would like to see the development of unions across Europe, since we are irrevocably tied up with it. The problems of global companies has grown, so it is important that the trade union movement across Europe at the least develops. Amalgamations across Europe are required, and I would like amicus to be an important part of that.

I would like to see the continuance of a Labour government, with it beginning to vigorously address the social question, the issues of equality and fairness. What do people really want from life – a decent job with pay, decent living standards, the chance to buy a house? I was talking to a taxi driver down here and he said that one of the local councils had a project to build affordable housing, and they were going for £400,000 each. Affordable housing? Who the hell can afford to pay that? The government should be working to create the climate so that people can afford homes.

There's other stuff like a world without peace, without fear, but that would sound like a party political broadcast. People want a job with prospects, decent housing, and when you don't have it most of the other problems like drugs emanate from that. I'm not one of those people who say that there are no bad people and that all problems come from society. I'm not a social worker. But society does create a lot of the ills.

If people had a job, reasonable living standards, if they could retire on a decent pension and have a house a lot of the ills could be alleviated.

Do you think capitalism can deliver all that?
No. No I don't. It's a force seeking to take out, not put in. You know

The Ragged Trousered Philanthropist. It explains how when it came to gas, electricity and so on the capitalists didn't want to make the investment so they had the Town Council do it. That's where 'town gas' came from. The capitalists couldn't do it themselves. You had the same with the railways, lots of little lines until the state stepped in, then you had British Rail. Now you've got the problem again, only it's not rail sizes or gauge sizes, its differences on safety, on service, rates of pay, on performance, all different.

Capitalism can't do it. It can't deal with society's problems, it only deals with the pursuit of profit. It shuts things down if they can't make money. Capitalists can't run the country, they can't run society.

5

Mick Rix

Mick Rix's roller-coaster ride as General Secretary of the train drivers' union ASLEF came to a surprising end when he was replaced in his job at the end of his five-year term in 2003. His election defeat represents the first electoral setback suffered by the left in the trade union movement in the last few years.

It is impossible to extrapolate broader trends from a single election in a very small, albeit industrially powerful, union. However, it is a measure of the extent to which ASLEF under Rix punched well above its weight in the wider world that his defeat attracted such attention. In a sense, the 40-year-old train driver from Leeds is the founding father of the 'awkward squad'. Certainly, when he was elected in 1998 there were no other union officials leading so consistently from the left. He has now handed the flame on to colleagues in far bigger unions.

This interview was conducted months before his election campaign, but retains its value as an outline of the thinking of the man who first put the 'awkward' into the squad. It cannot, however, address the reasons for his clear defeat by a right-wing opponent. Since I was an employee of ASLEF through most of the Rix years, I would suggest two major causes. First, important parts of Mick Rix's programme – a return to national pay bargaining for train drivers, active measures to address inequalities of gender, race or sexuality in the union and the industry, tackling institutional overtime on the railways and an emphasis on internationalism and an engagement with the wider labour movement – ran ahead of the views of many members.

Second, Rix's extraordinary run of industrial victories over employers – train drivers' pay rose by an average of over six percent every year of his leadership – earned him the undying emnity of very powerful forces in the railway industry and the establishment more broadly. These elements – the involvement of leading figures at the Strategic Rail Authority in the right-wing campaign was an open secret – organised efficiently to take advantage of the weaknesses mentioned above and on this occasion brought down their quarry.

At any event, the left movement in the trade unions may not hear much from ASLEF in the immediate future. But it will surely hear more from Rix, among the most intelligent, combative and principled union leaders of his generation.

How do you feel about being a foundation member of the awkward squad? It was given it's name at an ASLEF dinner at the TUC …

It started off as a piece of journalistic fun. I don't think that Kevin Maguire [Guardian *chief reporter*] knew what an impact his article would have. I think a lot of them have been embarrassed by the title, because most of them are modest human beings, very personable people.

We are just there to demonstrate our ability to carry out our members' mandates. But we are always open to other people's criticisms and judgements. I don't expect the media to be supportive and I think my other colleagues view it the same way.

We are all progressive, and there are some of us who want to promote a vision about how we want society changed, for the benefit of the people we represent. One of the things that has given me the most pleasure is working with Paul Mackney among all of the people who have been accused of being part of the awkward squad. He may not have endeared himself to the media because of his standpoint, being against the war from the very start, but he stands up for what he believes in. And he got re-elected as NATFHE General Secretary unopposed, which is a real testimony to him, because that union has a reputation of changing its general secretary every two minutes. But he did the right thing, and he's been supported.

Is there a new mood of optimism in the trade union movement?
There is a new leadership in some unions, and the rank and file are not so much defensive and introverted, more looking outwards to a bigger agenda that embraces social change. One of the reasons is that New Labour was elected on a real wave of public enthusiasm for social justice, to bring in changes. The vast majority of activists in trade unions do not necessarily feel betrayed, but they do feel that there has been a lack of action on key issues and are very impatient, very frustrated, with the pace of change.

After eighteen years of one of the most rabid right-wing governments in modern day British politics there are many issues which need to be dealt with. I don't think anyone could reasonably expect New Labour to wave a magic wand from day one, but on housing, welfare and other issues Labour got off to a really bad start by accepting for two years the spending plans of the Tories. That inhibited us going forward, even though the Chancellor may say it gave him a spending chest for later. But the government failed to tackle straightaway the social fabric, which was in urgent need of repair. No matter how little had been done at first it would have been a start, people could have seen that things were being started, and people could have been patient, waiting for more. But they didn't see the start.

Public sector pay is an example of that.

For eighteen years, or even further beyond, back to the Wilson–Callaghan years, workers in the public sector had been becoming more flexible, doing new things, but low pay was becoming the norm. There is something else in the pubic services, too. The vast majority of working people want nothing more than a secure life – money to pay the bills, have a couple of holidays, perhaps run a car, get out when they want to. They have a sense of working to live, not living to work. One of the underlying problems in the public services is the way they are treated, it is not just related to pay.

Public servants have a wealth of untapped experience which ought to be valued in the public service, but is not valued at all. Instead, they are always being told by ideologues that they should learn from the private sector, that the private sector can do it better. The public service ethos is about doing things correctly, about service to people, a human service. It is not just about quantity, about seeing how many people you can deal with in an hour, it can't be reduced to counting like in the private sector. So as well as pay, treatment of people is an issue. The main underlying cause of the trouble is the value placed on people in the public service. The contribution they make is undervalued.

Do you see that on the railways?

Well, we've been taught to believe we were in the private sector, now we're told that it's a public service being run by the private sector. If you want an example of how not to have the private sector managing a public service, it is the railways. There are some people who have done not at all badly out of the process, there is a lot of profit swilling around, but our people feel undervalued, there is no partnership process. People who work in the industry are treated as secondary.

There is no properly-funded staff training process, no schemes which could really enhance public service values and customer confidence. So many of those values have been eroded – lost – first by the run-down prior to privatisation, then by the privatisation process itself.

How do you get that balance between securing better pay and conditions, the union's core function, and delivering a public service, with that ethos you're talking about?

That is always the question we have to analyse. It is a problem which faces all general secretaries and leaderships of unions. I have been able to get pay and conditions improvements which could in some way be considered almost satisfactory, but I have been trying to keep the balance between an aggressive industrial agenda and maintaining an appreciation that you have to put something back into the industry and the service. That is where we always try and instill a public service ethos in whatever we do, but that obviously does not mean we are going to put up with low pay or poor conditions.

We are here to provide a public service. We know we could make the railways better if certain things took place. I believe trade unions are aware that you cannot move forward without an industrial agenda *and* a public service agenda, and there is no reason why you can't have both. I think most activists are happy with the balance and with what we are doing to provide further modernisation of the industry and quality public services. It's a difficult balance and sometimes we do not get the reaction from the membership that we want. But ASLEF is a union which believes in the public service we provide, in our craft, our professionalism and our integrity as a union. So we instill public service values, but never at the price of low pay and poor conditions.

Do you think the wider movement has the balance right?
I do not want to give the impression of preaching to other unions that the ASLEF model works best, but I think that one of the reasons we have had the successes of the last four years is that our approach is based on principles – the only way to win successes as a union is on a clear democratic basis and total consultation with the members. We believe that the rank and file should take as much as possible of the decisions in the union. That is a plus in itself, and we have to explain to the members the difficult balance, the responsibilities, that go with industrial muscle.

The strength of ASLEF is also that we have this very rigid discipline. No one can ever accuse us of breaking a deal, of going back on an agreement, once we have made our mind up. Everybody carries the agreement out, and if people are disgruntled, they can raise their point of view in their branch, at the conference, or in further negotiations. We offer total protection to our members, while working to make the industry successful as well. Sometimes we don't get the decisions right, but we make the best of it.

Whenever there has been a union as strong as ASLEF is, there have been employers trying to work out a way to break its power. Many in the privatised industry see the union as a dagger at their throat. Do you worry about anyone trying to take on and break ASLEF?
The thing at the back of my mind is that we have had a tremendous run of industrial victories, and sooner or later that is bound to come to an end if we are stupid. Personally, I think that the new movement as a whole is still too fragile, too young, too inexperienced. We cannot wipe away the bitter taste of eighteen years of reaction overnight. After five years of Labour there is some confidence that things are

changing. But it will take longer for new industrial activists to come through and get political understanding.

We cannot just rely on industrial strength, we need political influence. If we want to change the fabric of society that requires political influence, not just the industrial side. I hear clarion calls to do this, do that, and maybe twenty or thirty years ago we would have done, but society has moved on. I don't think people want constant conflict, they want to see fairness and justice, they want things to shift away from individualism towards a more collective approach.

But, yes, ASLEF is as vulnerable as anyone else, although we may have won a lot of victories. The forces that were there under Thatcher and Major are still there, they have not gone away. ASLEF on its own cannot beat the state. With the whole of the trade union movement, we could give the state a bloody nose, but I am not sure that the vast majority of members want to see that approach. What the majority want to see is a continuous advance to a better society and they want to achieve it without conflict.

Can it be achieved without conflict?
In my personal opinion, no, it cannot be achieved without conflict. Philosophically, I believe that the future could lead to a society where there would be no conflict. I believe that as a socialist. We should strive to make society less conflictual. That will happen when people are included and involved within the economic process and properly rewarded. But we are light years away from that scenario. I think when the movement is stronger, more politically aware, there may be a certain juncture where we will be on a collision course with those who have not delivered social justice and change.

How did you come by your own industrial and political education?
More than most people I was very fortunate to grow up in a family and a community where there was a lot of political activity. It was a very strong trade union household, so the values were instilled in me from an early age, but it was never beaten into me. I was taught to have an inquiring mind, to analyse and look at things. In terms of my working life, I started work for the nationalised industry, working alongside people who had fought for nationalisation, forty-five-year ASLEF veterans, who had all the scars of the battles of the past. What they instilled in me was patience, the way to advance is not by big bangs. They also taught me never to sit back on my laurels – you are only as good as your next agreement.

Good leadership and good trade union activism means always being able to learn, to see new horizons for those you represent.

Politically, I come from a left Labour and Communist Party background. A lot of my family were in the CP or on the left of the Labour Party – not just my father and uncle and aunts, but further generations back. I grew up listening to professors, scientists in the house, and I was never told to shut up, I was always given appreciation and encouragement to contribute.

When my parents went out, and I know this sounds really sad, but my baby-sitter was an active trade unionist, and when I was ten, eleven, twelve, my bedtime stories were quotations from Marx! When I look back I find that hilarious, although some people might find it depressing. Because of the capitalist system that we live under everyone goes through a time when they feel that they don't fit in, and I went through that when I was fifteen to seventeen and that was where my comrades and brothers in industry came in, especially ASLEF. My depot and my branch was very strong and active politically. Basically, it was run by the

CP. God knows how many copies of the *Morning Star* were sold each day. They were very, very good people. It will be very hard to replicate those sort of things in the near future. We will never experience the same social and working conditions because so much has changed.

Anyway, ASLEF instilled a discipline and a sharpness, and not just on issues which were transport or work-related. For example, I got interested in the peace movement. Sometimes, I think I am basically a pacifist, because I abhor violence. I know that it is complex and that sometimes it is a necessity. I think I would actually prefer to be a pacifist, but I've not come out yet! I have always been very interested in the peace movement. War threatens the total destruction of civilisation. Sometimes, I even think that the armed uprising of the liberation movements, which when I was younger seemed very sexy and attractive are not such a good thing ... it's very difficult.

When I got to Holbeck [*train depot in Leeds*] the CP was in total conflict and disarray, and the YCL was collapsing, otherwise it would have been expected that I join the Communist Party. I had a serious conversation with one or two other activists and it was decided that a lot of us would join the Labour Party on the basis that it was the mass party of the working class and that we should try and influence things. After all, the CP had twice tried to affiliate to the Labour Party and been rejected. At that time there were a lot of good Communists moving into the Labour Party. In my branch [*of ASLEF*] there were umpteen councillors, leaders of various committees, so it was not long before I was elected to Leeds District Labour Party and suchlike. I was twenty-four or twenty-five years of age when I started playing a large political role. The demise of the CP led to a lack of progressive knowledge within the ASLEF hierarchy. I was told I would never progress within ASLEF, which was not something I had thought about in any case. I was very happy living in Leeds. I loved the community I grew up in and to this day I miss the camaraderie of the workplace.

I was then approached by a senior officer of ASLEF who said that the union thought that perhaps I had the ability to become an MP. There were some people within the union who believed that that is where I will end up.

Will you?

I do not think that's possible. Why would I want to leave this job? There's only two ways you stop being general secretary of ASLEF – you retire or you get voted out of office.

Anyway, Leeds South and Morley was a constituency where ASLEF had a stranglehold and the MP was retiring, so there was a major move to push me forward. It was estimated that I had about 90 per cent of the union vote, and two of the local ward branches. Maybe the guy who won, John Gunnell, would have won anyway but I decided to pull out because of a tragic personal event in my own family. I had grown up on the principle of always putting the movement first, but there was a time when I had to concentrate on the family aspect.

What was the event?

I'd rather not say.

I became more and more in demand – I believe that was not just because of me but because of my branch. The local committee was a brilliant bunch. When we first brought women into the depot there was an immediate campaign for non-sexist behaviour, a welcoming attitude, a look at health and safety issues. Then there was the work I did with the Trades Council, and I used to get invited to Yorkshire NUM week-end schools, one of the few people from another union to be invited.

For three and a half years I went to all of them in Scarborough. But the essence of all this is I never had a proper formal education. I do not have an exam qualification to my name. I was very much self-taught.

No O Levels?
I only got a spirit level.

How did you come to pass through the Socialist Labour Party?
I had major reservations about the New Labour project coming to power within the party, and there were many people in the constituency who became disillusioned. Dropping Clause Four and the other alterations to the constitution and Party democracy were the last straw. Before, you could lose an argument but there was always room for debate, and you could put your case forward. But when they altered the constitution it meant that alternative ideas already had to have a certain percentage support; to even be discussed, it could take ten years to get a policy changed.

It seemed nothing could be done in terms of building a more accountable and democratic structure, so there were quite a lot of us who decided we were going to go off and join the SLP. There were a lot of good comrades who went that way and in the early months it seemed very good, a spirit of unity, with all walks of the left being involved at that time. But history repeated itself … I don't want to go into much detail about personalities involved, because I have a lot of friends in that organisation. But it was not going to be a mass party of working-class people and socialists. Also, things that happened during that time made it more difficult.

Then I was elected General Secretary of ASLEF and it was noticeable what short shrift I was given, and the things that were not said in my presence, and I felt the lack of influence a lot more. I believed that perhaps I had made the wrong decision in leaving and not standing my ground to keep the Party. There was also a lot of pressure from within the union to get me to join. I had a serious discussion with people, including Ken Cameron and Rodney Bickerstaffe, and they said it was in my best interests to rejoin Labour.

But what about the argument that Labour can't be changed, that New Labour can't be beaten? That is a tremendously important debate across the trade unions at the moment.

I was given a chance to come back. I knew I had made a mistake with my previous decision. I never wanted to leave Labour, but thousands of other people also did.

I personally believe, understanding the procedure, it is not as difficult as I believed to change the Party. It is achievable. Seeing another right-wing Tory government is one thing that really scares me to death. I want to ensure that that never happens again. I believe people want a Labour government, they want the Labour Party in power, but I believe they do not want to see New Labour in power.

That is my goal. I want to see the total removal of New Labour from my Party and if that means a total change in leadership, so be it. They have not brought forward social justice and they have not brought in social change for the vast majority of working people, who need it most.

Well, that's clear.

They know what I think.

6

Billy Hayes

If the postal workers ever go on national strike, it will no doubt fall to some miserable reporter on the Sun *to attempt to demonise Billy Hayes. It will be an unenviable task. The new General Secretary of the Communications Workers Union – another whose victory was against the odds, at least from the perspective of those outside the union – is a charming man of obvious decency. Thoughtful about politics and industrial relations, he is also passionate about the ordinary things – his family, music, football.*

He has to deal with Post Office management, which gives every impression of being the most inept in the country, at least in its handling of industrial relations, and with the privatised British Telecom. In a recent magazine article, he wove both Bertholt Brecht and The Clash into a narrative about the modernisation of the trade unions. He also wrote: 'The recently elected general secretaries share at least one thing in common: not to be wedded to the past. We all stood on a platform of greater membership involvement and participation. Supporters of "top down" methods have been swept aside. That is a warning to the government as well as a condemnation of many trade union leaders of the past.' [6]

You said something a couple of years ago that really stuck with me, about how good the 1960s were because you had a combination of The Beatles and Keynes and that made for a good life for working-class people …

I tell you my favourite illustration. I think it's right to say there's a revival in the trade unions. It may be a bit more hype than reality. It's like The Beatles and Oasis. I'm a big Beatles fan, although not because of the Liverpool connection, that never meant that much to me. Now Oasis sound like The Beatles, but without the depth or range that The Beatles had. When people say there's a trade union revival, it's in the same way that Oasis sound like the Beatles – it's true, but it's nowhere near the Winter of Discontent.

Strike days lost are nowhere near what they were in the 1970s, the late 1970s in particular. Our own experiences are an echo, an allusion, a reference, it's like you're sure you've heard this record before, which in the case of Oasis you have, because it's a steal. For example, in 2000–01 strike days lost in our industries were 0.2 per cent of the total. So it has to be put in that context. And in 1999 we had the lowest level of strikes recorded since 1891.

My thing is like 1960s stuff because for people of my age [*forty-nine at the time of this interview*], so-called baby boomers, post-war generation, those were halcyon days, in particular the 1960s. I was seventeen at the end of the 1960s, a bit young, which was a bit of a bind for me…

Too young to be a hippy, too old to be a punk.

[*laughs*] I was growing up in Croxteth, a council estate on the edge of Liverpool. It felt like a better period – there was full employment. The big thing there was getting a trade. You could read in the *Liverpool Echo*, there was columns, columns, columns of ships coming in. So there was full employment, a sense of optimism, The Beatles and all that.

The 1970s were the cusp of the militancy, of trade union strength, but getting into my mid-twenties we were getting into the downturn, then the miners' strike and on to the late 1990s. We had eighteen years of being hit, now we are witnessing a revival of sorts. You should not overstate it, but there is a revival. There was also the collapse of the Soviet Union and Fukuyama and the 'End of History'.

Now when I say a revival of Keynesianism would be good, I should say I've never read that much of Marx. But when I came down here [*CWU Head Office*] they were clearing out the library, getting rid of stuff and I saw they were throwing out the *Treatise on Money* and the *General Theory*, so I bought them up, 50 pence each. So I do know a little bit of Keynesianism, a little bit of Marx. I would settle for a bit of Keynesianism at this point in history, a bit of government intervention, government doing things.

What is our project? It is smashing the neo-liberal consensus, exemplified by the single currency and so on, that is what I am about. What I want this new group of trade unions leaders to be doing is to develop a new sort of alternative economic strategy.

I suppose the Marxist argument is that the ruling classes could afford Keynesianism in the 1960s, but in this phase of global capitalism and international competition they can't. Do you think they can?
Probably not in that sense. But what the left's project has to be is to develop a new consensus. I suppose Keynesianism is about the idea that the state intervenes on lack of investment. Our level of public sector investment is very low compared to Germany and France, particularly France. Government should be about doing things, about intervening in the economy. These are the rudimentary ideas that the left needs to be building on.

There is evidence from the communications sector. What should the union be doing? It should be about arguing for universal access – all citizens – even though we're subjects not citizens – should have access to letter delivery and to broadband, high-speed access. We have just one million subscribers to broadband, which is ranked in twenty-second place among Western economies, really poor. The neo-liberal idea that markets left to themselves will deliver benefits has been shown not to be the case.

Have you made any progress in convincing the government of this?
Let's take it sector by sector. The neo-liberal view of postal services is that electronic substitutes were going to take away this sector. But it's actually growing, mail volumes are growing, we can actually show that it's a growth sector – there is now more mail than there ever was. There were twenty-one million addresses in 1989, there are twenty-seven million now. So there needs to be investment. How are we doing with government? Not too badly, we have managed to get about £1.1 billion for the postal sector. It is going to expand further – we each of us get 343 items in the post per year, in the USA it is more than 700, so we can grow further.

In the telecomms sector, it is more difficult. But we seem to be making a bit of an impact with what is happening in broadband. We are also raising the idea of regulation. We would not necessarily have wanted regulators, but since they are here we are focusing on them being accountable. They are out of control. We got a resolution through the TUC about an enquiry into regulation. The sort of regulation we have is de facto privatisation of the decision-making process.

We are also showing that price cuts were made when the industry was under public ownership – more than since privatisation. The idea that public ownership is inherently less efficient is just not borne out by the facts.

The telecomms companies paid £22 billion for the G3 licenses. I was at a meeting, with the government there, when this guy from BT said it would cost £21 billion to cable up the whole country with fibre optic cable. He said, give us back £21 million and you will have the whole country cabled up and you'll still have £1 billion left over! But the BT guy was recognising that the issue needs government intervention. For broadband, government is the basic procurement arm. That is the idea we are pushing.

The theme is universal access, intervention and the renationalisation of BT. That last thing is not on the government's radar screen, to put it mildly. But we are trying to build a left consensus, with people to the right of me. That is possible if you have an interventionist agenda. For example, Demos has come out in favour of a not-for-profit telecomms network in the UK.

The trunk system, it's like trains. Mercury got access to it in 1982 and other companies want access to BT's local networks, but negotiating an entry price with BT is phenomenally difficult. So Demos is saying that the infrastructure should be owned by a not-for-profit company, same as the railways.

So we need to try and rebuild a consensus around these things. The new group of general secretaries, we have only just begun to feel our potential. We need a new alternative economic strategy, a new political philosophy.

Those eighteen years of defeats – how did that affect you personally?
I did not come from a great trade union background. The only person in my family who was active was my auntie, and she lived in Australia.

I was not politically active in any way. I was told by a teacher when I was ten that all the Liverpool dockers were Communists. That terrified the life out of me, as a good Catholic!

I joined the Boilermakers' Union. I went to the first meeting and there was Barry Williams [*a leading Liverpool Communist*] and about half a dozen others and these women from the British–Soviet Friendship Society who'd been invited. It scared the life out of me. I joined the Post Office in 1974 and it was a couple of years before I started to get involved. All around there were people saying 'I'll never go on strike again' because of the defeat the union had suffered in 1971.

But in terms of my activity, I had ended up in an industry that was expanding and, from 1979 onwards, was expanding phenomenally. In my time, I never experienced a major defeat as a union rep. The union – UPW, UCW, now CWU – never had the defeat the others did in that period, although it's not as true in the telecomms sector. I never experienced personally what the miners, the print workers, the dockers did. That has obviously affected our union. We have had setbacks, had trials, we never had a major defeat.

You had yours ten years earlier than everyone else.
The biggest strike I was ever in was 1988, we had national strike action for three weeks, and that was basically a draw. We had a strike in Liverpool that lasted ten days in 1985. Someone came down from head office, and decided he'd solved it. But we stayed out for another five days, in defiance of head office. So that is what shaped the union and me personally.

Then there was defeating Post Office privatisation …
That was a big victory, a bit of luck. Johnson led a good campaign

[*Alan Johnson, then CWU General Secretary, now a government minister*].
In the end commercial freedom for the Post Office was the solution.
It served its purpose at the time, but it's a bit of a millstone round our
necks now.

*Another important thing you've said is about the imagination and initiative of
working people just being ignored, never being tapped.*
Modernisation is a really Orwellian term. Like in Alice in Wonderland,
it means exactly what the person saying wants it to mean. What does
it mean? They assume that the workers themselves do not have the
imagination to think about ways of modernising the system, the
90,000 people who work in the Post Office do not have any idea
about how to improve the service.

The government's fear is that involving them will mean spending
on investment, it will mean resources. They do not want to tap into
the imagination because they are afraid it will cost them investment.

We are a producer interest, but we are not just exclusively about pay
and conditions. That is in a trade union's nature – we tend to be reac-
tive organisations. The left needs some kind of proactive agenda. Take
Back the Track, what Mick's doing, that is the way we have got to go.
It can't just be let's have more strikes. Workers are not stupid. They can
see that the Post Office has made £1.5 billion losses, that does affect
things. I have been involved in more industrial action than most, but
strikes are not a political strategy. We wouldn't be where we are now if
they were. What matters is having a worked-out political agenda.

*The Post Office has the reputation for having about the worst management in
the country.*
Money and conditions are obviously an important factor, but people

also want autonomy. They want a degree of autonomy and independence in their life, like you have and I have. When you have that, it is amazing how little they are off sick. If you do not have that empowerment, that is how it comes out. You see that in the Post Office big style.

Postmen and women have no autonomy. People may think they do, but it is all controlled. A lot of the strikes are about discipline and conduct more than pay. The government could improve things immensely – we often win reinstatement at Industrial Tribunals, but we do not get members their jobs back. If it was made obligatory for employers to offer reinstatement when it was awarded by the tribunal then, in the Post Office certainly, it would change things overnight.

You've said that one thing the 'awkward squad' have in common is moving away from a top-down approach in running unions. How's that working out?
The commandist approach is going out of fashion with trade union leaders. Greater involvement seems to be back in favour. People are expecting more egalitarian and democratic processes in society. People expect more involvement in the things they pay into, and that is exemplified in the trade unions.

In the workplace there is disillusionment with the neo-liberal, flexible market agenda and that is reflected in the elections taking place – top-down, that is finished; look at Simpson. In some of the companies where there is a no-strike deal workers will tell you that it's a load of tosh. What is the purpose, what is the point in being a member of a union? People don't want unions to endanger their job security, they want independence, but not damaging the company … it's a contradictory process.

The government is trying to roll back democracy – trying to end jury trials, freedom of information, etc. But now you've got twenty-four-hour news channels, they're business-led, but the technology makes it much harder to close things down like Florence and Genoa – it's carrying the seeds of its own destruction, its own gravedigger.

That's two quotes from Marx …
Is it? [*laughs*] Anyway, we're trying to make the unions more transparent. Keith Ewing is doing a study of how it should work – it is going to be quite critical of the union, building on the need for more openness, democracy and transparency, making the structures more meaningful.

You've also emphasised the need for unions to link up with other campaigns, other groups. That's been said a lot in the past, but little has been done.
We are participating in the European Social Forum – we have taken a stand as a national union to get involved. The problem you get a lot of is the 'what's in this for us' attitude. Unions tend to be very instrumental – you put in A and you get out Y. Now unions have got to invest for the future – we are supporting Catalyst [*a left-wing think-tank*] to get things out in the medium-term. After all, if we can't find a space for Roy Hattersley, we're not going to find much space for the awkward squad.

The TUC could do a lot more of that. For example, we had Charles Kennedy at Congress. Why not someone from the Greens, other organisations? Ideally, we'd like someone from the anti-war movement, but we're not going to get that. But we could get people from pension funds, pensioners' groups, women's organisations. There's a lot more of that we could do, even if we don't get immediate benefits. That's what the Greater London Council did, funding a lot of groups, that's one of the reasons why people look back on Livingstone's reign at the GLC as a good time. It would be different today.

Another thing is the property portfolio we have – think about how many trade union buildings we have, why not use them to assist each other in the localities.

On this instrumental point, how do you feel about the relationship with the Labour Party? Some argue that the unions are still putting in A and certainly aren't getting Y, or even N or P, from the link today.

We're quite clear on the link – we want to maintain and strengthen it. At this particular point in history, it would be a gift to the right. It's one of the things where the right and the far left agree with each other – break the link. It's incredible. The time is now to reclaim the Labour Party. We need to recognise that if the unions break from their historic partner it would be a backward step for the working class. More work needs to be done in the Party to strengthen the link.

My aim is to break the neo-liberal consensus. We have to defeat that in the Labour Party and the wider movement. If you broke the link, you would still be dealing with the same problem on the TUC General Council. My view is the left needs to create the same sort of consensus if it is to capture the leading positions in the trade union movement. I recognise the size and scale of the task.

What is happening in the movement with the awkward squad, is that some are trying to delineate us – he is more left-wing than him, they are trying to single Bob [*Crow*] out. We are not looking for traitors – but I would say that, I'm a general secretary [*laughs*]. The left tends to be hyper-critical of its leaders, but we're building a left leadership, working with groups that will help build a left consensus. You need that consensus – I do not think the working class will win just by striking.

You were very upfront in opposing the war against Iraq.
We took an anti-war position. I wrote an article called 'Give Peace a Chance', and took a firm position against the war.

But at the Labour conference some of our delegates wanted to speak against that position. There was massive lobbying from Nita Clarke, Charles Clarke, Sally Morgan [*all Downing Street or Labour Party officials at the time*]. They wanted to be able to say that Billy doesn't speak for the union. But we knocked 'em back. I've had no letters criticising the position I took.

7

Rozanne Foyer

Rozanne Foyer is an Assistant General Secretary of the Scottish TUC. Like much of the world, but unlike most interviewees in this book, she is young, female and not based in London. She has, literally, been a cover girl for new trade unionism. One of the first intake of organisers trained by the TUC's Organising Academy in 1997–98, she featured on the cover of People Management *magazine. Her organising placement was with the print/paper workers' union GPMU. After the Academy she returned to Glasgow to work for the STUC, which has traditionally been more engaged with the wider community and more left-wing and internationalist than the British TUC. Its General Secretary, Bill Speirs, has strengthened that tradition and Rozanne Foyer adds a considerable punch to it. Much of what she says may be as awkward to her colleagues in the trade union movement as it is to her opponents, but it can only be ignored at the price of missing the bus into the future.*

How did you first get involved in trade unionism?
I started working as a telephonist in the Benefits Agency when I was nineteen. I had worked since the age of seventeen in Customs and

Excise and I had hassle with a boss there, so I asked for a change of job and went to the Benefits Agency and it was there that I first joined the union, although I knew about unions because my dad was a train driver and a very active ASLEF member. But I became aware of the role of unions after being sexually harassed, when I got no support because there was no one there who was a member of a union, or at least no one had approached me about joining. But when I got to the Benefits Agency a union guy came to join me up straightaway. Then I started saying what is happening here, what is going on with this, so they said, 'why don't you become a rep, you do something about it'.

So when I became shop steward at that age, I was quite a freak! Then I was put on the branch executive, sent to conference – my branch was very good at supporting me. Then we came up for privatisation, all the support services – telephonists, cleaners, typists, security guards, messengers and so on. It was a PFI deal, done under the Tories, and all the support staff went with the property. The first time round the support staff won an in-house bid, but it had to be run like a private company. I ended up negotiating for 600 support staff in seven offices across Scotland who had been hived off, doing the negotiating with management at the age of twenty-one.

There were a lot of older guys around – Pat Kelly, the Scottish Secretary of PTC, Eddie Riley, the Deputy General Secretary, also Campbell Christie, General Secretary of the STUC, and Leslie Christie. They were called the Sauciehall Street mafia, and were quite radical for their time. So I got quite a lot of my politics in the pub at a young age, with all these big, really theoretical discussions. My wider political outlook I got from Pat Kelly and others on the STUC's youth committee. Until then I was involved in the public sector–private sector issue. I had joined the Labour Party because of that, and because I wanted to change the Labour Party and I naively thought that that was the way to get rid of the Tories. Cuts, health and safety issues, things like housing that I could see in my day-to-day work ... but the STUC youth committee got me into wider issues, international questions, wider equality issues, issues around poverty and social justice. So I became highly active within the Labour Party from the left. Now I am a member of the Campaign for Socialism within the Labour Party.

That is becoming a controversial issue now. Even among the new leaders in the unions there are two views – that there needs to be a fight to take back the Labour Party, or that it is a hopeless cause.

I am very much in the first camp. The unions have a much bigger role to play. There needs to be much more linkage with grass-roots Party activists. More union members are needed within the Constituency Labour Parties. The CLPs are sending right-wingers along to conferences. Trade union members should be activated to get their arses along to Labour Party meetings and have their battles within the Party – a real campaign for infiltration of the grass-roots. It only took Mandelson and Blair ten years to turn around the Labour Party. It is their intention to have CLPs run down and inactive. We have a much bigger job to do. Unions should be helping groups like the Campaign for Socialism and grass-roots members get along, start to articulate the arguments and not just wait for the union delegate to put up the arguments. For a time union leaders wanted to give New Labour a chance, brokering deals and backing off from a fight. Now we are getting ordinary Party members voting for more left-wing leaders, next we have to get the arguments pursued within the Party.

But how do you persuade people to do that, when the Party is so lifeless and the structures have been changed to squeeze out debate?

It is not easy. The right-wing wants to get on the gravy train, about getting people jobs. But there's only so many jobs to go round. Policy changes are our goal. In Scotland, at last year's Labour Party conference there was a situation where the trade unions finally got it together and said we will vote against the whole social policy paper because it was committing us to a massively increasing Private Finance Initiative agenda in Scotland. They lost the vote narrowly because the MSPs [*Members of the Scottish Parliament*] got the constituencies to vote against us because they said it would mean throwing the whole manifesto out. The CLPs had not been mandating delegates at this point, but we shall make sure at next year's Party conference that we do. We shall call meetings to discuss and debate the big issues and give our delegate a steer. So there are still opportunities to get the Party to change its course soon. I come from the Organising Academy, from a model of engaging members, which is not always what some unions want. Sometimes you march the members up the top of the hill, and they keep on going right over it ...

So what policy changes do you want to see in the Labour Party?

Top of the agenda would be the attitude to privatisation and dividing the public services. That has been a personal betrayal for me. That is why I joined the Labour Party because I saw the effect that it had had on people. It's not just because of what it has done to the workers, but also what happened when services are privatised, the standards of cleaning that have gone down at the hospital. I am really worried about the tax burden being passed on to the next generation or even the one after that, when they will have to build new schools and hospitals and we have still not paid for the ones we have now, which we don't really own.

It's like it's been on the railways, private companies just keep coming back to ask for more hand-outs whenever they want. Poorly-paid public service workers do not seem to get the same consideration from the Treasury.

Also I'm not so happy with the concentration on individual rights [*in employment law*] rather than on group rights. On equal rights, for example, big employers should have to hand in an annual review, prove that they are being fair, rather than individuals having to prove that they are not.

Then there is the whole international situation and I am very worried about a Labour government allying itself with the US in an ideological way. I would like to see it ally itself with Europe, which has a more social democratic tradition and agenda. My ideal would be moving our society towards the Scandinavian countries, where there is a higher standard of living, good public services, quite high levels of tax, but people understand what they are getting for it. That is where I would like to see our country heading, but we are going towards the US. Others started it, but Labour is following.

Some see the Scottish Socialist Party as an alternative to Labour in Scotland.
A lot of people disaffected from the Labour Party do find it attractive. The SSP has now taken over the Socialist Workers Party, which was the biggest active Trotskyist organisation in Scotland. The proportional representation system for the Scottish Parliament makes it even more interesting. They had Tommy Sheridan elected on the list system, and there is a Green Party member elected from Edinburgh. I think the SSP will actually grow in the next election, and get another couple

of MSPs. Smaller parties can table amendments and write bills in the Scottish Parliament, they are much more powerful as individual representatives.

Having the SSP there does push Labour to consider things, but it also leads Labour to oppose the most sensible things just because they come from the SSP. There was a debate around free school meals, but because it was an SSP bill, the Party was never going to back it because of who proposed it. So in some ways there is a backlash against the left wing.

I do not think the SSP will ever replace Labour. There is a conservatism in the Scottish people that means they will never go that far left. The SNP is the opposition, not the Tories, and they are a much more credible opposition than the Tories are down south. At a UK level the country is moving into war, there is the massive firefighters' dispute, the government is going into a head-on collision with public service workers. But in Scotland we have a different situation. PFI is far more attuned to what the unions are asking for, although of course we will never back it. Even the Tories agreed with free long-term care for the elderly when Labour was against it.

Joining the TUC Organising Academy at the very beginning must have had a big impact on your perspective ... I remember seeing your picture on the cover of People Management *magazine when the Academy started up.*
I really enjoyed it and learned a lot. I was pushed forward by the TUC quite heavily because they knew I had a background, knew about the politics around unions and could do press work, so I was pushed forward. Generally, it was a bunch of enthusiastic, campaigning people. There was a range of ages up to the late thirties, which is low in terms of the trade union movement. I was twenty-five when I went in, and

I had been doing trade union work for quite some time. We got taught quite radical ways of organising, and a model of empowerment that could be quite dangerous ... we nearly went on strike ourselves because some trainees were being treated differently to others.

I remember. I had been invited to give a lecture on communications but when I got there you were all in a strike meeting.

[*laughs*] It was a really interesting year. We were exposed to a lot of people coming to talk to us from the USA and Australia about the organising ethos. It is a way of thinking that stayed with us. I have brought it into the STUC – get people involved, not sit around talking about them. Don't leave it all to a full-time officer who may be like a second layer of management and doesn't talk to members.

In an organising situation, on greenfield sites it means finding new leaders, identifying issues that concern the workers, not going in to meet management until you have built up a membership, then present yourself as a union with an agenda, not as looking for a sweetheart deal and sign up the workforce afterwards to a deal you have already agreed with management. Some unions wanted organisers like that, but some trainees were simply sent to set up a stall in the canteen and give away free pens and insurance to get people into the union.

Without organising trade unions could die off, and you cannot deal with it by loading organising onto full-time officers who are already negotiating, dealing with individual grievances. They can't be expected to do organising on top of that. Simon, my partner, is a Unison full-time officer and even in the public sector, where union penetration is fairly high, he is always firefighting, dealing with grievances, on bullying cases, someone getting the sack. He has been taught the skills and techniques for organising, but he never has the time.

Why do you think unions have been so slow to grasp the organising agenda in practice? The theory has been talked about, agreed, for a long time now.

There are only so many resources unions have to go round. But they are not willing to break into their comfort zone and go out and organise. It's much harder to go out and get people activated, actually spend resources on organising rather than managing the organisation you already have. To do both is tricky. Empowering activists, giving them more power ... PCS and Unison are unions which are devolving a lot of responsibility to their local officials ... GPMU do not have that model. I know a GPMU shop steward, a convenor in a printing works with 1000 workers. He is not allowed to say 'boo' to the management without ringing up the full-time officer and getting him to come in and say 'boo'.

It's about power, about worrying that your members aren't going to go too far. It's not going to be easy for officers to shift the way they have been doing things, to go out and start organising and give responsibility to lay members to deal with some of their own problems.

On the point about resources, the amount devoted to organising is still very small, despite the fact that the neglect could end up being fatal.

Some unions do not want to change, do not want to use the organising agenda. But there are better examples...Tony Burke at GPMU is very evangelical about organising. He used to 'phone me at 11.30 at night to tell me about it. He was mad for it, which was a bit daunting at first. But he's just phoned me to say that GPMU have got recognition at Polar Cup, a big paper-making company. I had been used down there for six months, that was my placement. We built it up from five guys to eighty members, started running reps courses, drew up a charter of what the workers' wanted and ran a campaign in the local press against the Managing Director. We took a bus down there, and put placards at the end of the guy's garden. He was rabidly anti-union and there were all sorts of problems in the factory. That plant had 600 staff and it has taken two years to get to this point where we have union recognition. There are millions of places like that, where workers are having the piss taken out of them.

I was very pleased to hear Brendan Barber say that organising is one of his priorities. I hope that will really happen. With that lead from the face of UK trade unions, it could make a difference. This is not a left–right issue, it is absolutely vital. You will not get people organised unless you are out there campaigning, fighting for what they want in the workplace. That is how to grow the trade unions. That is my perspective for the trade union movement. It is not about what the General Council does, or doing wee backroom deals with the government. Members do not want that; they do not understand it; it is not what our job is.

I am for keeping the link [*with Labour*] but a link with teeth on it, a link which means something. We have to be very explicit about what we want from it. In Scotland, we had about five meetings with ministers in twenty years, now we have about five meetings a month with ministers in the Scottish Executive about transport, health, local government and education. We have got an agreement on a two-tier workforce covering all PFIs. In all future PFIs, workers will have their pension rights protected. What Blair has talked about, we have started doing. It is only because unions got access to the Executive that we pinned ministers down. We are still highly critical of PFI, there is no confusion about that, but every step towards workers' rights improving is a step forward.

The profile of trade unionism is still ageing. How can young people not born into a trade union environment, as may have been the case a generation ago, come to see the importance of unions?

At the moment we are talking to education ministers about the curriculum on aspects of citizenship, rights and responsibilities. We have said there should be something on trade unions in it, on rights and responsibilities in the workplace. I think that has got a bit to do with dealing with the problem. There are second or even third generation unemployed in the poorest parts of Glasgow. They have never been in unions, their parents never have, their grandparents haven't. When you get to that point you haven't any tradition.

We can't underestimate the impact Thatcherism had on our society, the damage to our community lives. It has been a massive change. Unions are something which clearly do unite communities, help rebuild them, so the idea of unions can be brought in that way.

The STUC has always been seen as pioneering that engagement with the wider community, far more than the TUC or any regional union bodies in England.

The STUC has been the voice of working people in Scotland on things like devolution, the poll tax, not just workplace issues. We have a broad social agenda, dealing with most social and political issues. When the Scottish did not have a parliament, the STUC was the nearest thing to it, speaking for Scotland. It got massive media coverage, had a real place in Scottish society. Since the parliament has started we have been changing our role. Now we have to deal with providing evidence to parliamentary committees, which demands lots of preparation and research, getting facts and figures, and we have to figure out how we deliver that. The STUC has to have a rethink about our role, which has changed radically since parliament came in. How do we make the most of the new opportunities? The job we did during the Tory years was a good one and a necessary one, but now a lot of it is less visible, done behind closed doors.

And we have to get the affiliates involved in this. For example, we were presenting something on 'best value' and how it affects equality and we asked the affiliates to give us details of sex discrimination cases, and they couldn't answer, they had no resources and we couldn't say anything that was not already available in the public records, which was useless. It's a massive waste of resources – why don't they send out a questionnaire to the members once or twice a year in a wee newsletter? Members are quite happy to fill in the forms and they feel in touch. I sometimes think that if unions are going to put resources into anything it should be into speaking to their members. If you are going to change anything politically, articulate arguments in parliament, then information from the members is like gold dust.

Finally, how do you feel unions need to change to become more relevant to women workers?
Should unions walk the walk, rather than just talking the talk? We are always going to look like dinosaurs until we do.

Getting to be a trade union leader you need to be an aggressive character, you need to shout down people at meetings, carry yourself with a bit of weight. It's quite a macho environment. More young women have been attracted to the New Labour type of leadership because the way it is packaged is more attractive. The whole of the union movement has a problem. We need more women at higher levels in the unions. In fact, the unions should hold their own equal pay review. I have seen so many brilliant, inspirational women driven out of the movement by men who want their position. They have been undermined, not protected, so they leave rather than stay on and fight.

The Scottish Secretary will always be a man, white and of a certain age. We cannot be taken seriously on equal rights in society, by government or even employers until we can make our own unions the way we want to see society be. Unions like Unison, GMB and the T&G, a massive number of their members are women, yet their regional secretaries are overwhelmingly men. This thing has got to be tackled, because we are not going to get away with it for much longer. It needs to change – at the moment we are a bit like the Catholic Church, always protecting their own. We cannot stick our head in the sand. How many times do you have to come up against sexism, and not be taken seriously just because you are a woman?

I developed a tough skin being a woman in the trade union movement, being a young woman. I could not believe the attitudes you came up against in the GPMU. I had to show that I could swear twice as much as them, become a wee hard bastard. It drains a lot of energy putting up that kind of a front, it wears you down in the end. You should not have to do it. We have fantastic resources in women, but we have not used the potential. And the unions at leadership level should not need telling what to do about it, because they have written the manual for other people.

I get really irate about it.

8

The Battle of Dolphin Square

If you were looking for the future of trade unionism, Dolphin Square might not be an obvious place to start. A world away from mine and mill, it is an imposing block of flats in London, just south of Victoria station, and home to the rulers, not the ruled. Peers of the realm, MPs, distressed gentlefolk and William Hague all make their home there. Princess Anne and Charles de Gaulle are among the former residents of 'Britain's most celebrated and salubrious housing estate'.[7] Dolphin Square has been the venue for a few notable episodes in history – Oswald Mosley was arrested there and Christine Keeler plied her trade in its luxury flats – but never in the history of organised labour.

However, the Square – the biggest housing complex in the world when it was built in the 1930s – was the venue for a strike in 2002 which had a number of surprising aspects. First, it happened in the notoriously hard-to-organise hotel and private services industry. Second, it united workers – mostly women – from all corners of the planet in a common struggle. Third, it was supported by most of the people who might have been most inconvenienced by it. And fourth, it got a result.

The 105 strikers were the back end of a classic 'upstairs, downstairs' division. The T&G had long organised the staff who, in endless corridors where the sun never shines – 'I still get lost after eighteen years coming here', says union officer Nick Page – keep the vast building running: the electricians, porters, cleaners and so on.

This gave the union a way in when the Square's owners turned part of the complex into a hotel. The hotel sector has been a booming element in the London (and national) economy for many years now and notoriously difficult to organise for trade unionism. Less than 10 per cent of the workforce are in unions, and that is certainly not on account of employees not needing union support in a sector well-known for low wages and management abuses.

But in Dolphin Square, the maids, porters and the rest were signed up to the T&G. Nick Page, sitting in the small basement office of union convenor John McCarron, takes up the story:

> The hotel gave us major opportunities to expand our membership base, out of the craft areas, into new areas. It also created a problem. No way would the company ever accept that the wages of those new members would be set by national agreements – the older membership had been tied to local government agreements.
>
> I negotiated with four general managers – they were usually ex-servicemen. They always said they would 'be mindful' of national agreements but that was it.
>
> The new members were mostly women. When the hotel opened most of them were Portuguese-speaking, from Portugal itself, or Angola and Mozambique. Now there are people from Eastern Europe, Lithuania, Latvia, Ukraine and from South America.

No doubt confident that this disparate group of women and men was not to be taken seriously as a collective force, management simply refused to accede to demands for a pay increase that would take its employees out of a poverty perhaps the more keenly-felt because it was being endured in the midst of not mere plenty, but excess.

Indeed, General Manager Adrian Wray told Nick Page that if the workers did not like the money they were being paid 'they can up sticks and go'. Since Mr Wray had previously complained that the union did not report properly to its members what was said in negotiations, this time extra care was taken to ensure that his words got back to the workforce verbatim.

'I conveyed this to the mass meeting and they went vroomph', says Nick. Mr Wray protested that his insult had been meant 'in confidence'. Poor man. After all, how many managers have said just that and worse during the 1980s and 1990s and got away with it.

So it was that, rather than upping sticks, the employees – including corridor cleaners, night attendants, health club staff and not forgetting the tealady (Flats Department) – voted to strike against Dolphin Square's low pay and military management methods. Pay started at just £5.41 an hour, with an average of around £11,000 a year. Bizarrely, management dismissed a claim for London weighting comparable to that paid in local government on the grounds that these miserable pay rates 'already reflected the property's location'.[8]

One chambermaid said 'we are totally underpaid and treated like slaves by a management that looks down their noses at us'.[9] One porter of Egyptian origin was dismissed (unfairly, as a tribunal later ruled) after a row provoked by his supervisor's habit of referring to him as 'Saddam'.

The first strike was set for 12 July. Nick Page: 'I woke up at one o'clock the night before. Would they actually do it on the day? We had never got near industrial action in Dolphin Square in seventy years. But when I walked round the corner, I saw twenty or so on the picket line. I thought "yes, we have done it".'

John McCarron continues: 'There were more the next day. We had to tell some of the women they could go, they stayed on the picket line for so long.'

The picket line, with every continent lying between the Arctic and the Antarctic represented, was interesting in itself. A young woman from Lithuania called Vilma – 'very trade-union minded, very internationalist' – was key to involving other women from Eastern Europe. 'And I saw a guy called Carlos on the line, and I thought to myself "you've done this before"', Nick remembers. 'I asked him if he had been on strike before and he said "oh yes, in Colombia, but this is a piece of cake, over there they shoot at you".'

The Dolphin Square pickets did not even draw the expected animosity from the well-heeled residents denied their tea from the Flats Department and other amenities. 'When we started the dispute our case was that we were representing working people on piss-poor wages in a classic class dispute with wealthy residents', Nick says.

But we got a terrific response from the residents. It was quite overwhelming. We only had one hostile reaction from a resident and he was pissed out of his mind – eleven in the morning and already gone. Labour residents were great, of course, like Lord Desai. William Hague just kept out of it – he's a lousy tipper anyway.

So at the second stage we modified our approach, and we had residents and workers making common cause. We had a meeting with the people who run the residents' association, dyed-in-the-

wool Tories, and there was a community of interest – they hate
the management as much as we do.

After two days of strike action, the dispute was settled for the
same increase as paid to local government workers, a considerable
improvement on the first offer, and a commitment by management to
a job redefinition exercise, which it is expected will lead to further
improvements. And there were less tangible gains: 'It has been about
self-empowerment, about the workers getting a sense of their own
self-worth', says Nick Page.

That struggle will be carried further in the job evaluation exercise.
'I am convinced that people have been discriminated against because
of their sex and nationality. People with exemplary records have been
passed over for promotion because they are not white, and the
composition of the workforce is not reflected in the number of women
in senior positions.'

All these are issues of the greatest importance to any union seeking to organise today's exploited workforce and deal with the issues
facing them. In London alone, there are hundreds upon hundreds of
Dolphin Squares, with low-paid, mainly female, often foreign-born
workers, labouring without any collective protection. There are no
more than pockets of union membership in the sector, mainly in the
GMB or the T&G.

And yet there was just one more surprising aspect to the story of
Dolphin Square. Leaving, I asked Nick and John if they had been
invited to give any presentations by the T&G or the wider movement
on the success of their strike. They looked momentarily taken aback.
'No', said Nick. 'You are the first person to come down and ask us
about it.' The dispute had been in July, and this was the end of

October. Not all surprises are encouraging. 'I did suggest to the region that they hold a one-day seminar on how to get industrial action', John added. 'I heard nothing back.'

Perhaps this is why his office was festooned with 'vote Tony Woodley' posters. The Dolphin Square strikers voted for the 'fight-back' candidate in the T&G leadership election.

9

Tony Woodley

After twenty years of defeats a little success goes a long way, and a big success has helped carry Tony Woodley all the way to the top of the trade union movement. He was the T&G's national secretary for the motor industry when BMW proposed to sell the vast Rover plant at Longbridge, for generations an emblem – perhaps the emblem – of the strengths and weaknesses of British manufacturing industry. The proposed sale to a consortium misnamed Alchemy would have led to the plant's closure and the direct or indirect loss of tens of thousands of jobs in and around Birmingham. Much of the movement – some within the T&G, indeed – and, of course, a Treasury wedded to free-market dogma, reacted to the news with an air of resigning to the inevitable. How many of the thousands of plant closures which have swept the length and breadth of the land since 1980 had actually been prevented, after all?

Woodley responded differently, leading a campaign which united the workforce and the wider Midlands community to save the plant, which was eventually sold to a rival Phoenix consortium, making cars and employing thousands on the site up to this day.

This victory propelled Woodley, himself a former car worker from Vauxhall's Ellesmere Port plant, to national fame. He was elected, surprisingly easily, to the

*post of the T&G's Deputy General Secretary in 2002 by a membership clearly
thirsting for the 'Longbridge approach' – fight back, don't sit back – to be spread
throughout the union. At the time of this interview, the T&G was waiting on
the impending retirement of Bill Morris. Woodley was a certain, if undeclared,
candidate in the election to succeed Morris and sit in the chair once occupied by
Ernie Bevin, Frank Cousins and Jack Jones. He won that election, too, of course.*

*The bare words on the page do not always do justice to the urgency, the
intensity, with which he addresses the problems facing the T&G and the wider
trade union movement. He talks about 'fighting back' a lot, which, coming from
him, is more than rhetoric.*

*You must be in a better position than most to judge if there is a new mood in
the movement, since you have been campaigning so much in the last year or so,
meeting people on the shopfloor.*

I think there is a real sense of disappointment amongst members that
the trade unions are less principled than in the past and do not seem
to stand up and battle for people's interests as in the past – that they've
become almost irrelevant.

Working people out there, because of the partnership principles
which have been adopted over the last decade and a half, purely to
give unions the chance of increasing membership, because of the
single-union, almost no-strike deals, feel that we have become part of
the management structure. And if that is the view coming from
people who are already in unionised workplaces, then I have to ask
myself, what do people who have never been in unions feel about us?

The changes go back to 1981 and 1983, to the Prior–Tebbitt
tranches of anti-union legislation. I remember a survey of 100 union
general secretaries about the ballots – I was a shop steward at the

time – and they said they had no problems with them. That was the start of the decline of union independence and strength in my opinion. Scaring us into submission was one thing, but it created a change among union leaderships – you know the saying, 'this would be a good job if it wasn't for the members'. It is an indictment about where we have gone since those days. There is cynicism, disillusionment and disappointment among our members. But now there is a rising level of expectation among our members, and the election of more forceful fight-back union leaders. Members are expecting more of us. I welcome that.

When unions are seen as part of the management structure ... it's quite an indictment. How do you start changing that perception?
Social partnership European-style is not really the issue. It really begins with the inward investment from the Japanese and the rush to get the deals done with trade unions. We have Japanese-model works councils, without the legislation providing for the influence which we have in other parts of Europe.

There is no doubt that this has seriously weakened grass-roots trade unionism. I would rather have a bilateral union deal with 80–90 per cent union membership than a single-union, almost no-strike deal with 12 per cent, which has become the norm in the motor industry, with Nissan being the first plant.

How do you set about reviving the grass roots?
After eighteen years of acquiescence to anti-trade union laws, with an inability or an unwillingness to fight back coupled with new agreements with works councils where you don't even have to be a union member, with many fewer shop stewards, the balance of power has

completely changed. If people think we were too powerful in the 1960s and 1970s, it is the opposite now.

But we should not be despondent. There is a new spirit of willingness to stand up to the guvnor, given proper leadership. Black and white, young and old, men and women, gay and lesbian all suffer from poor wages and bad conditions, and need a union as much as sixty years ago. Unions changed themselves, courted recognition from employers and weakened themselves – not terminally, but seriously. Now there's a change back. In the same way, I believe New Labour's days are over. They started by stealing the cloth of the Tories to get the Middle England vote, but ultimately, New Labour's day will come to an end.

What can the unions, the affiliated unions in particular, do to bring that about? Unions were founded to improve the lot of working people, of workers in struggle. That means campaigning industrially and politically on the big issues of the day. A big issue now is pensions; that wouldn't have been worth discussing thirty years ago, by our fathers. Now it's an issue, but for all our moaning we have not really started campaigning about it. It's about wages and conditions. That's what people want – they don't join unions for bloody free wills or half an hour free with a solicitor. They want a union to fight for them and they want protection when they are victimised and vilified in the workplace.

Unions have sometimes got a culture, under partnership principles, where, before they even listen to members' concerns they get the gaffer's 'moderate' view as to why our members should be sacked – there's a mindset that we listen to the employers before we get our members' point of view. Now we have Japanese working practices and new technology which means that our people are working harder than they've ever worked in their lives. At British Leyland we used to have 100,000 people, now there's about 10,000 and they're producing the same number of vehicles. There's a huge amount of wealth creation and fair shares are not being delivered to workers at the sharp end.

We have to stop concession bargaining and start fighting back. We have to let the members know that we are genuinely looking after their interests – they are told what unions are doing, but they cannot see our influence. You can't blame workers for not seeing what our value is, what our contribution is. That means standing up for our members, keeping them in work, stopping discrimination, getting genuine equal pay for women. I'm afraid the phrase 'back to basics' does come to mind.

Keeping workers in work has been one thing where there are very few examples of unions winning battles …

While capital is global and labour is local, we are going to be at a disadvantage. You have governments, never mind unions, that do not stand up to global corporations.

You need to get legislation that forces companies to have local content in products if they want to sell here. Capitalism will always go to the cheapest markets for labour it can to make the most profit. Global capital is already moving east, to China. At the moment we have completely unfettered control by global capital. Shareholder value will always be the law, and our members, our communities, our kids end up paying the price.

I believe we should create a legal framework to enforce not just shareholder value, but social values for the communities companies operate in. It may seem a pipe dream, but no more than some of the things the founders of the trade union movement were arguing for. Governments are not doing enough – it is stupid and irresponsible. They are elected and charged by the people in their countries with looking after them, but they are making the same mistakes as us. Government and unions have failed their constituencies and failed miserably.

What can be done to make companies behave differently?
How do you force companies to have a social conscience? It's difficult. I've never met a generous employer yet.

There's a part of industry that wants to sell in this country, but apart from that it's the global competitive agenda for profit only. We have got to give working people the chance to fight back, and international solidarity is incredibly important. You can't just talk about globalisation – it means the continuous abuse of our people, our plants and our country.

Other growing countries insist that jobs are created before there is investment in their country. China is doing it – they are saying if you want to come in you have to create jobs. When there is a market there, people are prepared to invest in jobs. It is for governments to say that if you want to trade and sell in our country, you have got to put something back. If you ignore it, there have got to be tariffs and penalties.

There are some decent companies, they're not all baddies. We have got to look after those people who show a social and economic responsibility and penalise those who do not want to uphold that level of decency. If they know it is costing them more they will think again.

Tony Blair said recently that the world was moving in one direction, and that was economic liberalisation.
Previous Labour prime ministers who would have been described as socialists would not have used those words.

Looking back to the 1970s, a critical thing was the unity of the T&G and the AUEW, Jones and Scanlon. Can you see that being recreated with Derek Simpson?

Size matters in trade unionism in my view. Jones and Scanlon were always walking down Downing Street. Did Ted Heath – or even Labour governments – really want them to be doing that? The fact is that they could not be ignored because they were the leaders of two massive unions which were involved in every element of the economy. They had to be invited.

Now it's an absolute necessity to bring together the new left leaders. This is not just about our own unions, it's about making life better for working people in this country. As I said before, I would rather have a two-union deal and represent all the members than have a single-union deal and represent a few. We are still, in spite of unemployment and so on, fighting over a membership that is not growing. We cannot keep competing for single-union deals by offering the lowest common denominator. I would welcome mergers, but the policies have to be right as well. Mergers with sensible, progressive unions, fighting for working people.

You mention amicus – if somebody had said to me that after the old ETU had effectively bribed its way to control of amicus, after they had got that old ETU culture in there, you would have had a principled left-winger like Derek Simpson, who is also a very decent man, that we could be allies, I would have said that that was beyond the realms of the possible. That unity is a realistic possibility that we cannot miss: growth, getting that industrial and political muscle, that must be our major aim and objective. Derek Simpson put his job on the line to become General Secretary, and I believe that I did under different circumstances, and we've not done it for personal glory or the House of Lords. We've done it to make a difference and if we

miss this opportunity and don't get somewhere then we will never
be forgiven.

*The T&G grew and became a force through both mergers and organisation.
Are you going to revive both aspects?*
There is no doubt that mergers and the extra finances will give the
T&G the platform to launch organisational growth, allow us to invest
at the grassroots and shop floor level, commit ourselves to going back
into the towns and cities which we have disappeared from because of
bare-bone economics. I believe small unions, like the miners now,
would be better served by amalgamation and using their finance to
become growing, community-based, more sizeable unions. How many
unions have merged into the T&G?

One hundred or so.
Look at the mega-mergers in companies – manufacturing, super-
markets ... it all affects unions. We will have fewer unions. We have
got to do more, bring more people together, we have got to stop
competing and start representing working people. The gaffers want
unions which are going to be acquiescent, weak and compliant, let's
not kid ourselves. Some want us to become business unions, but our
business is delivering real gains for our people.

*Looking ahead, can you see T&G, amicus, GMB and Unison all in one big
union?*
I remember sitting next to Sir Ken Jackson at a function a couple of
years ago and I said to him 'if the AEU and the T&G came together
we would have real influence, in motors in particular' and he said
'well, it could happen, there are no politics in this any more'. But there

lies the problem – there should be. If in Derek Simpson's nine-year tenure, or whatever he has left, he can model his union on his own principles and progressive background, then anything is possible.

And the GMB?
There is no place for two general unions. I don't feel that the new leadership there is opposed to merger or amalgamation. We should rule nothing out. We certainly have to have a union with industrial muscle. If you don't have muscle, you don't make a difference and nobody pays any attention to you.

Companies are merging across frontiers – do you think unions can? Or if not, what sort of international organisation is needed?
Well, the AEU have talked about that with IG-Metall. I said the same to Bill Morris and Jack Adams [*then T&G Deputy General Secretary*] ten years ago. But that's just spreading into Europe. The legislation governing workers and unions is so different; historically the unions are very different in each country. It's the hardest question you've asked me!

Going back to New Labour – how is that going to be dealt with?
If the present leader doesn't listen to what the ordinary voter is saying, doesn't listen to their values, and that threatens a Labour victory at the next election, then you change your leaders. Once you change the leader, like in a trade union, as happened with Derek Simpson, you can change the priorities, principles, direction of the organisation pretty quickly. The same applies to political parties. There are plenty of decent ministers and Labour politicians who have a real Labour and trade union history, and they will be ready to listen to the mood.

Obviously, the answer is not to have the Tories back. That is why I don't support breakaways from Labour, there is just no sense in it. So we need a real change of leadership to one that remembers the roots of the trade unions and Labour Party. There are people like Gordon Brown, but there are others, too, there are others.

Just look at Peter Kilfoyle and think about what he is saying. That shows how far Labour has gone. It's a great credit to him, he resigned on principle. He continues to battle for things that are important. Like me, his roots are genuinely at the grass-roots level.

You wouldn't have said that about him a few years ago.
Certainly not.

Can you convince the Party it needs to make that change?
It's about power, mate. Business leaders do what they think business needs, politicians will do what they think they need to do for power.

But have the unions done enough to stand up to New Labour?
Well, there was a euphoria for New Labour after eighteen years of the Tories. And in fairness the Labour Party has done things that we would have expected them to do in terms of investing in health and education. PFI is privatisation by the back door, and it should be resisted, but let's not kid ourselves, the Tories were winding up to completely privatise the NHS.

We have to get a balance here. It's about saying to Labour, you have stolen their [*the Tories*] votes to get into power, but don't steal their principles and move away from what our party was founded for. It will catch up with them, if it has not already done so.

I think a lot of this has been a bit negative, a bit doom and gloom. I'm a very optimistic person and for all the negativity, all the problems and disappointments. If we look at all the difficulties we have had to deal with, all the problems and the poverty we have had to deal with as unions, we have done marvellously well. It's unfortunate that because time has moved on, people do not appreciate that fully.

If we really become organisations that fight back for people, then I have no doubt that our future will be extremely bright. It's got to be – people depend on us.

10

Mark Serwotka

Few union election results caused more surprise than Mark Serwotka's elevation to the general secretaryship of the civil service union PCS. And no democratic vote has been more bitterly contested by the losing side. PCS, the end product of a long series of mergers between different civil service unions over the last twenty years, was under the leadership of Barry Reamsbottom, an aggressively right-wing figure who hailed from the old CPSA union. The CPSA boasted the most volatile politics of any trade union for many years, swinging violently from one election to another between a hard-line cold-war right and a left heavily influenced by the Militant Tendency.

Reamsbottom did not contest the election which saw Serwotka win a surprise victory over Hugh Lanning, on one view because he failed to secure sufficient nominations to do so. Serwotka, following his election, became General Secretary-Designate, scheduled to take over in spring 2002 when Reamsbottom would retire. An agreement was signed to that effect. But when the appointed moment came Reamsbottom persuaded the PCS executive, on which he had just secured a majority of his supporters, to accept suddenly-produced legal advice to the effect that Serwotka's election was unlawful and that the incumbent – himself – could remain in office for another two years.

This manoeuvre provoked outrage amongst the PCS membership and, eventually, a High Court ruling that Serwotka's election and the subsequent retirement agreement signed by Reamsbottom were valid. It was a squalid end to Reamsbottom's leadership, but a very difficult start to Serwotka's.

Serwotka came to office direct from the shopfloor – in his case, the Benefits Agency in Sheffield. He was never a paid official before being elected General Secretary. His opponents suggested he did not have the experience required to manage the large budgets of a major trade union. But he has perhaps more relevant experiences for leadership: 'I worked for twenty years administering benefits in a DSS office. I experienced all the issues that our members have to put up with: low pay, lack of staff, bullying management. I also had experience of how ineffective my union was in fighting for members', he says. He has declared a break with 'social partnership' in the conduct of PCS business. 'Some people believe that the way to grow unions is to reach accommodation with many employers. I want a greater understanding with employers, but it's the members who come first, and this is the philosophical divide', he told Red Pepper.

Serwotka is clear that his approach is different. 'I am still seen as an activist. People want radical change, they do not want to tinker. They want a complete change of approach, and they want us to articulate their disgruntlement with government.'[10]

He is also unusual among the new leaders in being an individual supporter of the Socialist Alliance, the electoral grouping established by the Socialist Workers Party and some tiny far left groupings to challenge Labour at the polls. This interview, conducted as war raged in Iraq, focused on his views about the political future of trade unionism.

How do you think Labour–union relations stand at the moment?
First of all, from a PCS perspective – government is the employer of our members so we are uniquely placed. There is an enormous

disappointment among our membership about the fact that things are not changing in the area of privatisation, that things are actually worse.

There is a strong tradition in the civil service unions of standing up against the employers – now that means standing up against a New Labour government. In 1997 a majority of our members voted Labour for the first time. Now there is a profound disappointment. So the path that I have steered with the government is very popular with the members, because it means standing up to the government.

On the wider front, there is no consistency – CBI on one issue, the TUC on another. The proposals on a two-tier workforce in local government were good, but the next week the government sided with the CBI on employment law, not even changing the eight-week rule dismissing strikers who have gone through all the legal hoops.

As for the attitude to the public sector, it has not changed with a Labour government. More money has been put in by Gordon Brown, but it has not gone to the workforce – much has been creamed off by the private sector. We have people earning under £10,000 a year, some of the lowest paid people in the country. We have the issue of privatisation, where we have had promise after promise made before 1997, on air traffic control for example – remember 'our air is not for sale', privatising the maintenance of the royal warship fleet by the MoD. All things described by Labour in opposition as insane to be done by the private sector, but all carried out by Labour in government. For example, 65 per cent of all security guards in government buildings are now in the private sector, with appallingly low pay.

It does not seem that there is a political relationship with the government at all. This explains, I think, the rise of elected left officials and the leftward move in many unions. People see the unions as the real opposition now.

So what should the unions try to do about New Labour, that is the question really agitating people now?

The industrial unity of left union leaders has to continue. It would be a tragedy if a split occurred on the issue of the Labour Party. People in the TUC and the Labour leadership want to sow that division.

But I believe that there needs to be a left-wing alternative to the Labour Party, but we are not at that point – we are miles from it at the moment. But the achievement of the Scottish Socialist Party in seven years is incredible. They could take four to eight seats [*in the May elections for the Scottish parliament*] – a big step forward. In England and Wales we are nowhere near that position.

Unions which are affiliated to the Labour Party have a different issue to people like me. I am not going to tell those unions what to do. They have been affiliated to the Labour Party for a hundred years, that is a massive issue for them to consider.

We are balloting to have a political fund next year. If that was pitched around the Labour Party, we would lose. That is why we intend to have a real discussion about what we should do. I do want to take the debate forward without splitting anyone. I hope a way can be found for those fighting within the Labour Party to be supported, and those currently outside may be able to attract support from those people in the Labour Party. There was the recent meeting which George Galloway spoke at – there was an overwhelming unity from a packed meeting. The feeling is – this is not a slogan – that we must be able to support people within the Labour Party like John McDonnell and Alan Simpson, but not people like David Blunkett and Barbara Roche. There are people in the Labour Party we can support and those we can't support. The detail of how we can carry that forward is the critical discussion.

As for the unions that are affiliated, there are differences emerging. RMT may be making a different decision to ASLEF or the CWU. What would allow the left to break out of its small, embryonic state? The Socialist Alliance in its present form is likely to change and is likely to broaden, increase its base among trade unionists, people fighting in the anti-war movement.

Individuals can of course pick and choose between which Labour candidates they support or don't, but affiliated unions aren't in that position.

That is one of the difficulties – one of the downsides of fighting inside [*the Labour Party*] is that you have to back the lot. You have to look at how it can be done – supporting Ken Livingstone was a difficult one, but it was managed somehow. In Scotland, FBU members are standing in opposition to Labour. RMT may support John Marek in North Wales, and an RMT member is number three on the SSP list.

I think there are thousands of trade unionists and some of the leaders who will support candidates who are not Labour candidates. Some of the distrust of breaking with Labour is the fear that it could lead to apolitical trade unionism, which is the last thing we want. We want a political voice which really represents trade unionism. If you live in Scotland, you can vote for the SSP. Until there is a real alternative many people will stay put. Can the trade unions play a role in this alternative?

There is a danger of the fragmentation of the political labour movement, isn't there, if some unions do one thing and others another?

In changing times, things do not always move as one as we would like. There is a real danger that if nothing is done then in five years' time things will be exactly as they are now and that would be unacceptable.

I see the danger of a drift towards the US political model. We have to develop change, and that will be necessary, and if you do not start somewhere you are never going to progress.

I think there will be splits, but at the moment less than half the TUC membership is affiliated to Labour. As much industrial unity as possible has to be maintained, but we will have political differences. If some unions are in the vanguard of that and carry things forward, and at the same time others are behind, then that is inevitably the way we progress. There are some people who tell me sincerely that the Labour Party is on the verge of being won over by the left. I do not see that – more people are leaving than joining.

The anti-war movement was a tremendous opportunity. Yes, there is a possibility of fragmentation – there is fragmentation when progress is being made, rather than in five years when things are still as they are now. I do not argue that everyone should leave the Labour Party and break the link, but I do welcome the debate about what we need to be doing.

Do you believe that the Labour Party is done for?
Yes. [*pause*] I can expand if you want. [*laughs*]

Perhaps better say where you think we could be five years down the line.
It has to be linked up with the issue of proportional representation. The SSP would not be winning eight seats if there was not a PR system. PR would allow for alternatives to register, so there has to be a discussion around that.

But in some ways it is impossible to predict. You have to look at George Galloway's position in the Labour Party – some people are talking about leaving, some are talking about staying and fighting. And who knows the outcome of the war? The Prime Minister could still be toppled, which could open up new possibilities. The post-war period could also see new attacks on trade unionism and union rights, and big disputes.

At the time of the next election I would like to see parts of the country where there is unity on the left to support candidates who are opposed to Labour, while in others we would support left Labour candidates. It will not be easy, but I would like to see credible candidates that are a springboard. The conditions that gave rise to the SSP are different, but people said it was the wrong way to go. Now, with 15 per cent of the vote in the polls, to say to them 'go back into the Labour Party' would be inconceivable.

That is where I would like to be in five years. Will we be there? Who knows. This is the most interesting political period I think we have been in for the last decade. I would rule nothing out at the moment. George Galloway had this quote from Lenin: there are decades when nothing happens, and there are weeks when decades happen, which shape decades to come. We are in one of those periods.

Do you see the anti-war movement as having particular potential in this respect?
Absolutely. Anyone who took it for granted would be foolish, but anyone who did not see its potential would also be foolish. Two million marchers, appalled at the government going to war without any legal or moral justification – my guess is that many of them do not want to vote Labour again because of what they have done. These people need an electoral way to express themselves – that is the potential.

But I know that politicians who attach themselves to movements are resented. We need a painstaking way of debating and drawing out the logic of this. It has huge potential, but we must proceed carefully.

Ultimately, the Socialist Alliance was about a bringing together of left groups, and important as that is, it was a big step forward, it has not broken out of being seen to be an organisation of the far left. A political alternative is never going to be based on the revolutionary left coming together. It has got to be massively bigger than that.

What do you see as the key issues around which that alternative could be built?
Seven million trade union members must be the starting point and their policies. That means a decent minimum wage, bringing back privatised services, tackling poverty which, despite Gordon Brown's protestations, is still a real problem in this country.

We also have to deal with fundamental social issues like crime and housing, which the BNP is using. People are voting for them in Labour areas – people have to feel that the left, as well as the right, have answers.

This should all be addressed by a real rise in taxation. Companies that make billions are avoiding tax, they should be forced to put more in. It would be a very popular programme.

It's one thing to list the policy demands, which would certainly be popular, but to launch a serious party there has to be a broader sense of identity which people relate to, since most voters never read the detailed manifestos.
It's a very difficult question. I was brought up in the South Wales valleys – people did not give a toss about the manifestos, they just voted Labour. Breaking into that is very difficult. In South Wales people are protesting against Labour by voting for Plaid Cymru or by not voting at all. More did not vote. Breaking into a decades-old historic allegiance is a massive job.

My view of that would be that you will break through by being the people who put the most deprived first. It could be about the NHS, or about decent pensions for many people. The key point is that we are the fourth richest country on the planet, we must be able to do more than we are managing at the moment. It is not a snappy election slogan, but it is a positive, not a negative. People are constantly being told, we can't do this. We have to say: 'yes, we *can* do this'.

I suspect that the sea change we are talking about means getting on the first rung of the ladder. In Scotland they are already on the second rung, but in England we are not on the ladder yet.

You are emphasising bread-and-butter issues, which is how the SSP built itself up, but the anti-war movement has been more focused on peace and democracy as key questions.

Yes, there is a feeling that this country should be seen to be one with a progressive outlook, rather than just supporting the USA and getting dragged into wars. There are many in the anti-war movement who are not ready to vote for a hike in taxes for example, so we have to look at the immediate issues.

Couldn't it work the other way round, mobilise people on the issues of peace and democracy first …

The anti-war movement is a vast, vibrant campaign – look at the school kids it has brought forward, it has people who are well-off, who may have voted Tory or for the Liberals, who may want to vote for peace and democracy, but have not talked about more fundamental issues like taxes. But we can all agree that we are disenfranchised at the moment, we can all agree that the government does not speak for the people of this country. The real question is: is it inevitable that these people want to pursue issues with the left? It will take a long time and a lot of political discussion.

Gordon Brown does link the two issues, doubling the war budget at a stroke while not having enough money for other things.

Absolutely. We have got to break out of seeing alternatives just as the creation of the far left. There is a danger if people within Labour start attacking those who are outside, and conversely create a sectarian approach among those who are outside Labour. Can that logic be broken? There are hopeful signs.

There should be real targeting to create a credible alternative. In Hackney, for example, no one could dispute that Paul Foot's campaign for Mayor was serious. He came third, just behind the Tory. Labour got far more, but you could not say it was irrelevant. Yet in another election the Socialist Alliance got two hundred votes against twenty thousand for the Labour Party. Barbara Roche, for example – there is no reason why a credible campaign could not be fought there [*Hornsey and Wood Green*] with a high-profile candidate. It would be wrong to stand six hundred candidates – target them so they are not seen as fringe candidates.

We are talking about the long term. It is vital that those seeking to offer an alternative do not just parachute into a constituency and disappear. They need to be involved in local campaigns and become a permanent feature of political life. Scargill appearing in Newport, then Hartlepool, it's not serious. You need to be painstaking in getting support in the community.

It will be very interesting if some of the MPs who supported Blair on the war are deselected by their constituencies, but they are told by HQ that they cannot do it and constituencies are closed down. Do they fight on within the Labour Party, or do they do something else?

This position has been described as pessimistic. It is not pessimistic to create an alternative.

But isn't the big problem that if we go down this road we end up with all the socialists over here and all organised labour, or most of it, over there, and that reverses the main achievement of the creation of the Labour Party, which was to bring socialism and labour under one electoral roof. Separate socialists without organised labour are sterile, and labour without socialists are pragmatic and limited.

That's very vividly put, very well put. It is drawing out the problem. Organised labour includes many individual trade unionists who have made the break and they are not involved. I think that some of the unions that are defending the link are doing so at the cost of distancing themselves from their own shop stewards. If in five years' time you have ten thousand socialists here and the unions maintaining the link that would be a step backwards. But I suspect there will still be socialists in the Labour Party and trade unionists who stand outside.

If people inside support candidates outside, they risk expulsion. But I expect the Labour leadership would have to think long and hard. I do not want to be where your question suggests; that danger has to be at the back of people's minds.

In the past, you had to be in or out, there was no middle ground. But now we are beginning to see that it does not have to be like that. George Galloway is talking about people inside and outside the Labour Party. He wants to work with people who want to reclaim Labour for its values. At a rally like that, you could be split down the middle after two speeches and everything could disintegrate if one was saying everybody must be in [*the Labour Party*] and the next was saying you must all be out. You have to work together – the first hurdle is always the highest, but that is what you have to explore with people.

Conclusion: Truth and Order

A strong trade union, bent on self-interest and rejecting all self-reform, is an enemy of political order and economic truth.

Hugo Young, *Guardian*, 25 November 2002

Perhaps *Guardian* grandee Hugo Young is right when he sees strong trade unions as a natural enemy of 'economic truth and political order'. By the former he presumably means the market economy, and by the latter the suffocating political consensus that sustains its domination of every aspect of life. Even without an explicit commitment to seek an alternative social system to capitalism, trade unionism doing its basic industrial job is bound to rub up against these end-of-history shibboleths. The biggest change in the last couple of years is that a growing number of union members – and nearly all their newly-chosen leaders – are explicitly aware of this.

The truth-and-order defended by Young and most of the rest of the establishment has produced a deeply unequal and unstable society, polarised between rich and poor to the detriment of any sense of community, and which celebrates avarice and individual acquisitiveness. It dangles great prizes before millions, yet denies to most any hope of attaining them. As one service after another is privatised, the pitiless march of commodification reaches almost every corner of life while every other human connection is allowed to 'dissolve into air'. This transformation is held to be unchallengeable, imposed by forces – 'globalisation' or 'international community' – without an address to be lobbied or a leader to be called to account. More than ever, the mass of people are left to dangle alone, their sustaining communities of work and location upended, and the state provision for times of need squeezed pitilessly – again in the name of an 'international competition' from which none may abstain.

It is not surprising that all this reaches its clearest expression in the world of work. It is here that the inequalities are generated and the instability enshrined. The 'job for life', or even the middle-class 'career path', which could be taken as a measure of dignity and security, a foundation for individual development, is now a ridiculed notion. Even the prospect of retiring on a decent pension seems more elusive – the deferred wage represented by pension contributions is now, by government order, to be deferred to a moment much closer to death than anticipated. The rhetoric of 'flexibility', favourite mantra of New Labour's ideologues, means casual work, limited rights, no certainty, the employee forever at the mercy of extraneous and unmanageable forces. The only sure way to stability in working life is through joining the small number at the top who, by grabbing as much as they can as fast as they can, at least ensure that they always have a well-stuffed pillow for a soft landing, should 'flexibility' require it at some time or other.

To build a vibrant and positive trade unionism while accepting the parameters of such a system and society is, over time, a labour of

Sisyphus in which, as Bob Crow puts it here, everything that is gained one year is likely to be taken away the next. Of course, things can be achieved here and there, particularly when the capitalist business cycle is on the upswing. British trade unions could surely have a couple of million more members simply through better work, and more imagination, while changing nothing fundamental in society. Beyond that, beyond the point where organised labour simply regards itself as one pressure group amongst many, competing to have its sectional demands heard by those who magisterially determine what is and what is not in the 'national interest', lies the issue of power.

Everything trade unionism does is about power, starting from the recognition that power is inherently unequal between the employer and the employee. Combination is the acknowledgement of this and the first step towards redressing it. Everything a trade union does – contesting the speed of the assembly line, the length of the working week, the lower rates of pay for women, the exclusion of black workers from skilled jobs – is, to some degree or other, an argument about power, about whose priorities and values prevail, about who is in charge here.

That much is widely accepted in the trade union movement today. The idea of a 'social partnership' which could obscure the power question is more discredited by the day, not so much by force of argument as by the bare reality of society, and the limited achievements secured by imagining that sweet words and good intentions can make the imbalance of power irrelevant. The more important question is this – at what point does the dispute over power, over control, stop? As an argument over who dictates what happens within the workplace? Or over whose workplace is it anyway? Or, in the words of Bertholt Brecht, at the point where you have to ask 'whose tomorrow is tomorrow – whose world is the world?'

That is the question that strikes at the heart of the debate about the future of trade unions. A particular union is inevitably a sectional interest. But the cause of labour as a whole cannot be reduced to pressure-group politics. The values of trade unionism – solidarity, equality, community – should form part of the common culture of society; and it is not a coincidence that social cohesion has frayed in Britain in step with the decline in trade unionism. Trade unionism has often sold itself short ideologically, but it embodies much of what the vast majority of people want from the organisation of the world around them. As Gregor Gall put it, 'trade unions are, no matter what their faults and imperfections ... by far and away the most democratic, representative and inclusive of all organisations in Britain. They hold out the possibility not merely of democratising and civilising society as a whole, but in particular bringing representation to the grossly underrepresented and ignored.' Perhaps that last sentence should be turned around. Unions cannot merely bring representation to the ignored, but they can change society as a whole. That is why they are still feared by those who cannot countenance any such change, be they Tory or New Labour.[1]

Some of what unions stand for is derided as the special pleading of the 'producer interest', opposed to the 'consumer interest'. The text here is that it is only as consumers that people can express themselves and enjoy a rounded human existence – work is merely the dull and dehumanised dead time necessary to enable us to exist as full and free consumers at weekends. This is a philosophy of self-mutilation, one which degrades the creative and social potential of work, where we spend most of our time, and exalts the limited and passive experience of most consumption in its place. The alternative is not to reverse the balance of power and exalt 'producer' over 'consumer' – syndicalism, which commits each industry or workplace to the exclusive steward-ship of those employed in it, is an ineffective means of articulating the interest of society as a whole. A progressive trade unionism which aims to humanise work cannot but challenge the producer/consumer dichotomy and help underpin a more fulfilling and integrated view of human potential both at work and outside it, and lay the foundation for the extension of such values throughout society as a whole. It cannot but be political.

The vice that has beset the British labour movement for a century and more has been pragmatism, a denying of politics and a lack of perspective beyond bread-and-butter issues. Rejecting such pragmatism does not mean ignoring the obligation to reach agreements with employers which leave the realities of power unchanged – every union has to do that on those innumerable occasions when there is no serious basis for raising any more fundamental point. The 'pragmatism' which hovers like a reproving elderly relative at the shoulder of every struggle is the one which accepts our world as it is, which celebrates every partial gain as, in effect, proof that the worker need never worry about his or her status in society, about being the ruled but never the ruler. Such pragmatism today means above all failing to explicitly challenge the private monopoly on wealth and power – that is what Bob Crow means when he argues here that 'trade union politics is bourgeois politics'.

For example, we can be pleased that the Labour government has changed the law to make winning trade union recognition much easier. But what is the value of such a change when an employer targeted for recognition can say – and several have – that if they are forced to concede they will simply close the affected workplace and relocate operations overseas? It is only by confronting the issue of their exercise of this power with the threat to take it away from them that the labour movement can trump that ace. In industrial relations and society too, a level playing field is the one which has only one player on it.

Essentially, this is an argument for a new socialism. There is no reason to be shame-faced about that. Every facet of life shows not only the desirability of an alternative way of living, but also the difficulties trade unions encounter when they let the logic of their work and struggles stop short of that objective.

What, after all, lies beyond New Labour? Not, let us hope, a return to Toryism. There is little appetite in the country and still less in the working-class movement for that, although the spectre will certainly be conjured by those who demand that we cling on to New Labour for fear of something worse. This is a moment of great encouragement, when the practical alternative to the policies of Blair and Brown comes not from the right, but from the left, from the spirit and policies of a resurgent trade unionism, articulated by a leadership of socialists.

In that sense, the 'awkward squad' is a new twist on a deep-rooted historical movement. The very first TUC, in 1868, saw a debate between the advocates of subordination to the needs of the employing class and those who believed the new movement had a world to win, between the respectable and the radical.

And it was sober British trade union leaders in the 1860s – awkward before their time – who gladly put their names to the endeavour to 'convince the world at large that their efforts, far from being narrow and selfish, aim at the emancipation of the downtrodden millions … if the trade unions are required for the guerrilla fights between capital and labour, they are still more important as organised agencies for superseding the very system of capital rule'.[2]

Superseding capitalism? It will certainly be awkward, but not as much as tolerating it.

Notes

Part One

1. *Financial Times*, 25 November 2002
2. *Guardian*, 27 November 2002
3. *Sun*, 26 November 2002
4. *Guardian*, 29 November 2002
5. *Magnificent Journey* by Francis Williams, London: Odhams, 1954, pp. 12–13
6. *British Political Facts 1900–1979* by David Butler and Anne Sloman, London: Macmillan, 1980, pp. 330–31
7. *The 1945–51 Labour Governments* by Roger Eatwell, London: Batsford Academic, 1979, p. 54
8. *Dancing with Dogma* by Ian Gilmour, London: Simon & Schuster, 1992, p. 72. The average annual growth rate of the British economy during the eleven years of Mrs Thatcher's premiership was 1.8 per cent, during the preceding eleven years it was 2.6 per cent.
9. Williams, op. cit., p. 13

10. *British Trade Unionism* by Allen Hutt, London: Lawrence & Wishart, 1975, p. 244
11. *The Rebirth of Britain* by Wayland Kennet (ed.), London: Weidenfeld and Nicolson, 1982, pp. 43–44
12. *Straight Left*, September 1980
13. See *State of Siege* by Jim Coulter, Susan Miller and Martin Walker, London: Canary Press, 1984
14. *Red Pepper*, September 2002
15. *Conference Report*, London: Transport and General Workers Union, 1996
16. *Election Address*, Derek Simpson, 2002
17. *Guardian*, 22 November 2002
18. *The Times*, 27 November 2002
19. *Daily Mirror*, 2 January 2002
20. TUC press release, 9 March 2002
21. *Independent*, 31 December 2002
22. *Guardian*, 6 December 2002
23. *Progress*, August/September 2002
24. *New Statesman*, 17 September 2002; *Financial Times*, 9 March 2002
25. *The Times*, 3 April 2002
26. *Guardian*, 4 December 2002
27. *Guardian*, 23 November 2002
28. *Union Futures* by Jane Willis, London: Fabian Society, 2002, p. 17
29. TUC press release, 20 March 2002
30. *Union Innovations* by Unions 21, London 2002; Paul Donovan in the *Morning Star*, 24 December 2002
31. TUC press release, 27 November 2002
32. Author's notes

33. TUC press release, 18 April 2002; *Financial Times*, 29 May 2000; *Progress*, August/September 2002

34. *Election Manifesto*, Tony Woodley, 2002

35. *Guardian*, 27 December 2002

36. TUC newsletter, 1 November 2002

37. Willis, op. cit., p. 2

38. *Revolutionaries* by Eric Hobsbawm, London: Abacus, 1999, p. 260

39. *One World, Ready or Not* by William Greider, New York: Touchstone, 1998, p. 415. Greider's suggested solutions to the problems of the world economy of the 1990s are actually rather mild, but his analytical sweep, and his assembly of information, are outstanding. I was so enthused by his work when it was published that I bought copies for three colleagues, all leading figures in the trade union movement in Britain. When I checked six months later, none had so much as opened the book!

40. *Union Revival – Organising Around the World* by John Kelly, London: TUC, 2002

Part Two

1. *Financial Times*, 16 April 2003; *Guardian*, 18 April 2003

2. *Sunday Times*, 20 April 2003

3. *Red Pepper*, September 2002

4. *Financial Times*, 30 December 2002; *The Times*, 19 December 2002

5. *Guardian*, 15 July 2002

6. *Red Pepper*, September 2002

7. *Independent on Sunday*, 14 July 2002
8. *Caterer and Hotelkeeper*, 11–17 July 2002
9. *Morning Star*, 20 July 2002
10. *Financial Times*, 28 January 2003; *Red Pepper*, September 2002

Conclusion

1. *Scottish Left Review*, January/February 2003
2. *Instructions for the Delegates of the Provisional General Council to the Geneva Congress of the International Working Men's Association in First International and After* by Karl Marx, Harmondsworth: Penguin, 1974, pp. 85–6

Index